DATE DUE

ƒ⌐c			
GAYLORD			PRINTED IN U.S.A.

TOBIAS SMOLLETT
TRAVELER-NOVELIST

TOBIAS SMOLLETT
TRAVELER-NOVELIST

"Vlysses, the long Traueller, was not amiable, but eloquent."—NASHE *The Vnfortunate Traveller*

By GEORGE M. KAHRL

1968

OCTAGON BOOKS, INC.
New York

Reprinted 1968
by special arrangement with the University of Chicago Press

OCTAGON BOOKS, INC.
175 FIFTH AVENUE
NEW YORK, N. Y. 10010

LIBRARY OF CONGRESS CATALOG CARD NUMBER: 68-22295

Printed in U.S.A. by
NOBLE OFFSET PRINTERS, INC.
NEW YORK 3, N. Y.

PREFACE

IN RECENT years travel books have rather superseded
the classics as a happy hunting ground for scholars,
but, unlike the classics, they have seldom been read as
literature, although from the days of Howell, Burnet, and
Addison many have been written by English authors distinguished in other literary forms. Furthermore, travel books
have been séarched as historical and biographical documents,
as the sources of other books, while their proper qualities and
literary merits have been neglected. A full history and criticism of the literature of travel has yet to be written, nor is
this the occasion. The following pages, however, had their
inception in two observations made regarding the role of
travel books in English literature.

Early in my studies I discovered that many English travelers were as enjoyable and rewarding as some of the poets, es-
sayists, and novelists. The travelists not only set down a
wealth of factual information; they often wrote with undeniable grace and made many original observations on the per-
ennially absorbing subject of man's adjustments to diverse
environments. Also I found a peculiar affinity between
novelists and travelers, it not always being easy to distinguish
one from the other. The rapport between the two began in
ancient times and among the romancers and picaresque
writers, while in England the traveler and novelist were combined in Defoe, Fielding, Sterne, Scott, Dickens, Thackeray,
Barrow, Marryat, Trollope, Stevenson, Bennett, Kipling,
Conrad, Hudson, Lawrence, and Huxley, to name only a few.

Tobias Smollett is an early and excellent example of the
novelist-traveler or the traveler-novelist, who, like the writers just mentioned, wrote both prose fiction and a book of
travels. The present study is concentrated on the bearing
Smollett's travels and his acquaintance with the literature of
travel had on his prose fiction. Since the study by no means

v

embraces all of Smollett's life and work, the conclusions are necessarily limited. They do not touch all his attainments in prose fiction, nor do they offer a key to a full appreciation of his art; but it is to be hoped that out of this study will grow a new understanding of Smollett's sources, his milieu, and his powers. For much of his best prose fiction he drew upon his own travels, not in the spirit of an autobiographer, but in that of a traveler describing conditions and scenes of contemporary life at home and abroad. He often followed the traditions of travel literature in subject and form, and it was with the spirit and purpose of a traveler that he wrote many of the passages in his early novels and almost all of *Humphry Clinker*. He was a born humorist; yet travel may have given his spirit a predilection or bias for the humor of the external world—the humor that appeals to the senses, that laughs at human customs. His comparisons are more original than his interpretations; his accuracy and objectivity, even his Scottish prejudices, more acceptable than his plots and sympathies. He brought to prose fiction the interests, habits, and methods of the traveler and thereby gave to the novel what it has so often lacked and without which the imagination labors in vain—a broad and critical observation of human society.

I am fully aware of the vagueness of my title and the arbitrary division of the chapters, but the pursuit of a versatile and restless Scot on a subject whose only unity is personal or geographic does not lend itself to exact definition or co-ordinate proportions. The creative mind does not follow an outline, and to anatomize its resources by too rigorous a system defeats a grasp of the creative process. If classification has, therefore, been subordinated to analysis, it has been necessitated by Smollett's far-ranging mind and the indiscriminate curiosity of travelers. I can only hope that the digressions will be no less interesting now than they were to Smollett and that ultimately I shall succeed in guiding readers back from the bypaths to the highway—to a richer enjoyment of Smollett's prose fiction.

It is a pleasure to acknowledge the generous assistance I

have received. To the late Professor Chester Noyes Green-
ough, under whom the study was undertaken, I am grateful
for wise guidance and cordiality. For the privilege of repro-
ducing the illustrations by Rowlandson I am indebted to the
Widener Memorial Library of Harvard University and to
Professor Edward L. Hubler and the Library of Princeton
University. At different times I was aided in the preparation
of the manuscript by Miss Mary Hagopian, Mrs. Madeleine
Gleason, Dr. Marie Edel, and Miss Anne Steele. For assistance not acknowledged in the footnotes I would like
to thank Professor Edward S. Noyes, Dr. Luella F. Nor-
wood, Dr. Lewis Hanke, and, in particular, Professor Lewis
M. Knapp, who through the years has been most generous to
me, as well as to other students of Smollett, and who has been
good enough to criticize the whole manuscript. Finally, in
preparing the material for the press, I have been encouraged
and assisted by Professors Hyder E. Rollins, George Sher-
burn, and Tom Peete Cross, all of whom read the manuscript and suggested numerous corrections and changes. For
their many kindnesses I am most grateful.

Nor must I forget my hospitable friends for many sum-
mers in Cambridge, Dr. and Mrs. J. Butler Tompkins of Bel-
mont. Publication has been made possible by the thoughtful
generosity of the late Miss Anna Jessup of Aley, Syria, a
sturdy critic of good books. Though she often regretted that
"of making many books there is no end," I can only hope
that, were she alive, she would approve of one more. Great
praise is due my wife that she bore so long with good-
humored patience the "bubbly-nosed callant with the stane
in his pouch."

G. M. K.

Kennebec Point
September 1, 1944

CONTENTS

LIST OF ILLUSTRATIONS

BIBLIOGRAPHICAL NOTE

Shortened titles are used throughout this book for the following biographical sources. As listed here, their order is chronological.

MOORE, JOHN, M.D. *The Works of Tobias Smollett, M.D., with Memoirs of His Life* (1797). Edited by JAMES P. BROWNE, M.D. London, 1872.

ANDERSON, ROBERT, M.D. *The Life of Tobias Smollett, M.D., with Critical Observations on His Works* (1796). Edinburgh, 1803.

SCOTT, SIR WALTER. "The Life of Tobias Smollett" (1821), in *The Miscellaneous Prose Works of Sir Walter Scott*, Vol. III: *Biographical Memoirs*. Boston, 1829.

CHAMBERS, ROBERT. *Smollett: His Life and a Selection from His Writings.* Edinburgh, 1867.

HANNAY, DAVID. *The Life of Tobias George Smollett.* London, 1887.

S[ECCOMBE], T[HOMAS]. "Tobias Smollett," *The Dictionary of National Biography*. London, 1885–1901.

NOYES, EDWARD S. *The Letters of Tobias Smollett, M.D.* Cambridge [Mass.], 1926.

The following are the texts to which all references are made:

The Works of Tobias Smollett (prose fiction only). Edited by GEORGE SAINTSBURY. 12 vols. London, 1895.

Travels through France and Italy. With an Introduction by THOMAS SECCOMBE. "World's Classics." Oxford, 1907.

"Account of the Expedition against Carthagena in the West Indies," edited by W. E. HENLEY and THOMAS SECCOMBE in Vol. XII of *The Works of Tobias Smollett.* New York, 1901.

The illustrations by Thomas Rowlandson are reproduced from:

Peregrine Pickle. Edinburgh and London, 1805.
Roderick Random. Edinburgh and London, 1805, and Edinburgh, 1809.
Humphry Clinker. Edinburgh, 1809.

INTRODUCTION

FROM time immemorial travelers have embellished their tales with fiction, and storytellers have enlivened and strengthened their narratives with travel, to the confusion of historians and geographers but to the delight of readers. If travelers did not people cities with children of their imaginations or rear up mountains in the deserts of old maps and dot their routes with monstrous beasts, their books would be more often consulted but less read. In Herodotus, in the cosmographies, in the stories of Marco Polo, Prester John, Mandeville, John Dee, and Thomas Coryate, and a long succession of other actual or imaginary travelers fact and fiction were so mingled that Misson's *New Voyage to the East-Indies* (1708) and Defoe's *Captain Singleton* (1702) were accepted as genuine, while Ctesias, who "left unnoticed many things far more marvelous than any he has related," was in the end to Photius "only an arrant story-teller,"[1] and James Bruce, whose *Travels To Discover the Source of the Nile* (1790) is one of the great books of African exploration, was identified by contemporaries with the then celebrated Baron Münchhausen.

Swayed by popular taste, rhetorician and redactor fathered upon Alexander the Great a mass of fabulous ethnography and natural history, first on India and the East and later embracing most of the travel lore of the ancient world, until Alexander was fairly crowded out of the legend. Quite typical was the attitude of the author of the Middle English *Kyng Alisaunder* who, once he had Alexander across the Indus River, paused to remark:

> Lete we now Alisaunder in pays ride,
> And speke we of wondres that ben biside;
> Listneth of wondres, and sitteth in pes.[2]

[1] J. W. McCrindle, *Ancient India as Described by Ktêsias the Knidian* (London, 1882), p. 34.

[2] Henry Weber, *Metrical Romances* (Edinburgh, 1810), I, 3–327, ll. 4850–52.

It is not surprising that the legend of Alexander the Great as compiled by Vincent de Beauvais became a fruitful source for the *Travels of Sir John Mandeville*.³

Mandeville's anticlerical guide to the Holy Land recalls the countless books of missionaries, pilgrims, and saints who seasoned a pious record of devotion with perils in Myrmidonia or Scythia or in the heart of darkest Africa. An excellent example of the fusing of vernacular voyage material with a saint's life is the *Navigatio* of St. Brendan, surnamed "The Navigator," who, to judge from the eighty extant manuscripts in several languages, was known all over Europe.⁴ He was an Irish monk at Clonfert who died in 577 or 583 but did not come into his own until the ninth or tenth century. Now back of the *Navigatio* was an Irish *immram* or prose story of an adventurous voyage, the *Voyage of Malduin*.⁵ In the redaction St. Brendan replaces the Irish adventurer and goes himself in search of the other world, or *insula deliciosa*, with, to be sure, the appropriate ecclesiastical interpretations at every turn. As to his motives for voyaging abroad, one Latin text briefly remarks, "Deus voluit tibi ostendere diversa sua secreta in oceano magno,"⁶ but a Low Saxon with more originality enlarged upon the motive thus:

> Having read a book full of miraculous stories, so strange and incredible, [St. Brendan] waxed indignant at such extravagancies and threw the book into the fire. Then God, to punish his incredulity, commanded him to forsake his country—to take ship and traverse the wide ocean for seven

---

³ *Mandeville's Travels*, ed. P. Hamelius ("Early English Text Society," Nos. 153 and 154 [London, 1919, 1923]), II, 19–21; Sir George Frederick Warner, *The Buke of John Maundeuill* (London, 1889), Introduction, p. xxiii, and notes; and Albert Bovenschen, *Untersuchungen über Johann von Mandevile und die Quellen seiner Reisebeschreibung* (Berlin, 1888), pp. 206–306.

⁴ For a discussion and full bibliography see James F. Kenney, *The Sources of the Early History of Ireland* (New York, 1929), I, 406–20, and "The Legend of St. Brendan," *Transactions of the Royal Canadian Society*, XIX (May, 1920), Sec. II, 51–67.

⁵ Heinrich Zimmer, "Keltische Beiträge II Brendans Meerfahrt," *Zeitschrift für deutsches Alterthum*, XXXIII (1889), 129–220, 257–338, and St. John D. Seymour, *Irish Visions of the Other-World* (London, 1930), pp. 69 ff.

⁶ C. Wahlund, *Die altfranzösische Prosaübersetzung von Brendans Meerfahrt* (Upsala, 1900), p. 98, ll. 13–14.

years, that he may see, with his own eyes, those wonders, and greater than those wonders, he deemed so unworthy of his belief.[7]

Never was a skeptic more punished by the knocks and perils of traveling than was St. Brendan, but for the reader, now as in the Middle Ages, the center of interest in the *Navigatio* is the unnatural history and geography which survives almost unchanged from the pagan originals. As Professor Kenney in his study of the legend concludes: "The author or authors drew freely from the resources which the geographical knowledge, the literature, and folk-lore of Ireland and of western Europe offered, and shaped all with care to his own purpose. The *Navigatio Brendam* is the epic—shall we say the Odyssey? —of the old Irish Church."[8]

The fictitious or fabulous elements in travel books are slight compared to the prose fiction that travel has fostered. Utopias, imaginary voyages, and fictitious travel letters, the mere cataloguing of which is the task of a lifetime, have long been the stock-in-trade of philosophers, journalists, and needy authors. Even more numerous than the imitators, however, have been the sedentary authors who borrowed from travelers to lend a realistic or romantic quality to prose fiction. Ultimately back of much classical and vernacular fiction is the remolding of a historical figure into a legendary hero, and, in conformity to the age-old and universal archetype in the epic, the popular imagination has elaborated the travels. Odysseus was made to toil ten years along the shores of the ancient world before he reached his home in Ithaca, only that Homer might include all that was known of the Mediterranean. Apollonius of Rhodes, re-working the legend of Jason into the *Argonautica*, concentrated so much on Jason's travels that in the end geography became the principal ingredient of the epic. In the *Aethiopica* Heliodorus car-

[7] Rev. Denis O'Donoghue, *Brendaniana* (Dublin, 1893), pp. 71-72. See also Charles Plummer, *Vitae sanctorum Hiberniae* (Oxford, 1910), I, 103-7, also p. xli, n. 2; Arthur C. L. Brown, "The Wonderful Flower That Came to St. Brendan," *Manly Anniversary Papers* (Chicago, 1923), pp. 295-99; A. Jubinal, *La Légende latine de S. Brandaines* (Paris, 1836); and Karl Schröder, *Sanct Brandan* (Erlangen, 1871), pp. viii-ix.

[8] "The Legend of St. Brendan," *Transactions of the Royal Canadian Society*, XIX, 67.

ried Theagenes in pursuit of Chariclea from Greece, to Syria, and finally to Ethiopia, bolstering the extraordinary with natural history and geography clearly appropriated from travel books. Achilles Tatius inserted in *Clitophon and Leucippe* lengthy accounts of the hippopotamus, elephant, phoenix, and the spring where one fishes for gold. This pattern of the voyaging hero who must before he dies visit the far corners of the earth, often to be deserted on some distant shore while the author digresses on beasts and fowls, floods and mountains found only in books, became the universal model for fiction in later centuries. Arthur was carried to Rome, Charlemagne to the East, Ivain to the land of the Torelore.

Later, with the revival in France of the heroic-romance, Gomberville in *Polexandre* defended "tous les lieux où il semble que la vray-semblance est mal obseruée" by citing the geographers "depuis Ptolomée iusques à Christophle Colomb." Accepting the form and subject of classical romance, Gomberville undertook to inject a new reality into the tradition, not simply by appealing to the imagination or ideality and ancient authority, but by verifying ancient fables with modern geography and utilizing material from recent explorers.[9]

The antiheroic or picaresque tale also profited by the universal appeal of travels and voyages. Originally picaresque romances were antiheroic only in the social status of the antihero and the milieu in which he moved. In form the tales were modeled on the loose, episodic framework of the romance prototype with its digressions and peripatetic adventures. Apuleius established the genre as a satire on the various grades of society when he metamorphosed his antihero into a donkey and sent him wandering from master to master in rural Thessaly. Centuries later Mendoza in *Lazarillo de Tormes* and Le Sage in *Gil Blas*—works generally accepted as the purest forms of the picaresque romance—recounted

---

[9] Marin le Roy, sieur de Gomberville, *Polexandre* (Paris, 1637–38), pp. 1332–87. A full and acute discussion of *vraisemblance* in the heroic romance is to be found also in Madelène de Scudéry, *Ibrahim ou l'illustre Bassa* (Paris, 1641), Vol. I, Preface.

the experiences of a humbly born servant who in his travels from master to master learned to know bakers, priests, innkeepers, beggars, lawyers, doctors, petty thieves, and squires, only to laugh at them.

Mindful of popular relish for criminal biographies, some authors subordinated the servant to enlarge upon the rogue and his sundry tricks. Alemán in *Guzmán de Alfarache*, Lópes de Ubeda in *La Pícara Justina*, and the anonymous author of the *Vida y hechos de Estevanillo González* all expanded the theme of roguery; and, in England, Thomas Nashe, apparently unaware of *Lazarillo de Tormes*, approximated the picaresque tale independently when he wrote *The Unfortunate Traveler*, the autobiography of the rogue Jacke Wilton, who for only a part of his travels abroad is the servant of Henry Howard, earl of Surrey. Other well-known English examples that merged the picaresque romance with the criminal biography were Head and Kirkman's *The English Rogue*, Captain John Stevens' *The Spanish Libertines*, Defoe's *Moll Flanders*, Fielding's *Jonathan Wild*, and Smollett's *Ferdinand Count Fathom*.

In other hands the antihero was stripped of his servant-rogue characteristics and transformed into a restless young man, often of good family, adventuring and traveling in many parts of the world. Espinel's *Marcos de Obregón* is the story of a worthy but poor esquire who must make his own fortune. In Gonzalo de Céspedes y Meneses' *Varia fortuna de soladado Pindaro* the central figure is a soldier of fortune; in Sorel's *Histoire comique de Francion* he is a young and gallant adventurer; in Scarron's *Roman comique*, a young actor; in Fielding's *Joseph Andrews*, a servant discovered to be a gentleman; in Smollett's *Peregrine Pickle*, the spoiled son of a retired London merchant. It is difficult to draw the line between what is picaresque and what was only inspired by the picaresque, but careful readers will agree that, once the antihero ceases to be a rogue-servant, the result is no longer strictly picaresque. Certainly Le Sage in *Le Bachelier de Salamanque* and *Les Aventures du flibustier Beauchêne*, Chetwood in *The Voyages and Adventures of Captain Robert Boyle*,

Defoe in *Captain Singleton* and *Robinson Crusoe*, and Prévost in *Le Philosophe anglois, ou histoire de Monsieur Cleveland* preserved only the traditional adventure-travel framework of the romances while introducing a new type of hero and a new milieu. As a group these writers were widely acquainted with the literature of voyages. Prévost, for example, had a hand in a twenty-volume *Histoire générale de voyages*, and he sought to imitate the authentic voyages so closely that his fictions, now recognized for what they are, would be accepted as genuine. As a follower of Defoe and Le Sage, Prévost expressed the point of view and illustrated the methods of the groups as a whole when in his "editorial" Preface to the *Histoire de M. Cleveland* he wrote:

> La *Colonie Rochelloise* m'a causé de l'embarras. Il ne me paroissoit pas vraisemblable qu'un Établissement si extraordinaire eût été si entiérement ignoré, qu'il ne s'en trouvât nulle trace dans les Relations de nos Voyageurs, & je ne pus m'empêcher d'en témoigner quelque chose au Fils de M. Cleveland. Il me satisfit aussi-tôt, en me faisant voir quelques endroits d'une Relation de la Mer d'Ethiopie, composée par *William Rallow, Anglois*. Si je n'y trouvai point l'Histoire de *Bridge* & de ses Compagnons, je fus assuré du moins de l'existence de la Colonie, & de la maniére déplorable dont elle fut détruite. J'y remarquai même quelques singularités de sa situation, que M. Cleveland avoit omises, & que j'ai jointes à son recit dans le troisiéme Tome.[10]

The picaresque novel affords two opportunities for the inclusion of travel material. As the rogue-servant passes from master to master, he often travels from country to country. In the Spanish novels he not infrequently is captured by Algerian pirates, and, before returning safely to his native home, he sees much of Africa, Italy, and the Mediterranean. In the second place, to escape the penalties of the law, he often flees abroad, whereupon the reader is treated to a comparative study of the manners of several countries. Jacke Wilton is ever at pains to distinguish the English from the Italians; Lazarillo also passes much of his time among the Italians; Cervantes, remembering his own captivity in Algiers, inserted the story of Gìnes de Passamonte in *Don Quixote;* and, before he returns to Naples, Estevanillo has

[10] *Le Philosophe anglois, ou histoire de Monsieur Cleveland* (London, 1777), I, xvi–xvii.

traveled over Spain, Italy, France, and parts of the Low
Countries, Germany, and England—the widest range of
travel in Spanish picaresque fiction. The French imitated
the Spanish in sending their picaros to Italy, Spain, or Algiers,
and the characters of Defoe, Fielding, and Smollett are no-
torious rovers.

In one respect, however, writers in the picaresque tradition utilized travel material with a difference. Unlike the romancers, who projected their stories into countries remote in
time or space, the picaresque writers emphasized the contemporary and the immediate and consequently were more
detailed in their descriptions. The point is too obvious to re-
quire illustration. The explanation lies not only in the fact
that the authors were describing the contemporary scene but
also that they were autobiographic to a greater extent than
other writers of prose fiction. This was true even in ancient
times, for Apuleius' *Metamorphoses* is now generally considered to be more autobiographic than any of the other
relics of ancient fiction. The most famous example in Spanish
literature is *La Vida de Marcos de Obregón* by Vincente Espinel, which Don Juan Pérez de Guzmán in his edition of
1881 demonstrated to be, with the exception of one episode,
an accurate biography of the author. Another interesting example is *El Viaje entretenido*, written by Agustín de Rojas
Villandrando and recounting the experiences of a troupe of
traveling comedians in Spain. De Rojas' work in turn suggested the even better-known *Roman comique*, by Scarron,
in which the author described his acquaintance with "La
troupe du Marais" that passed through Le Maine on its way
to Alençon in 1638, when Scarron was a *chanoine* there.[11]

Among eighteenth-century writers, ever aware in theory
and practice of their literary antecedents, the long and
varied service of travel to prose fiction was common knowledge. In their hands the traditional relationship was emphasized and elaborated. Literary sophistication alone, however, does not fully account for the intimate relation of

---

[11] Henri Chardon, *La Troupe du roman comique dévoilée et les comédiens de Cam-
pagne au XVIIᵉ siècle* (Le Mans, 1876).

travel and prose fiction during the eighteenth century. More immediate causes are to be found in the ever increasing number of Englishmen who traveled the world and in the extensive literature of travel that pervaded the intellectual atmosphere of English life. It is hardly necessary to run over the names of the circumnavigators of the globe, the voyagers and travelers to India, Africa, China, the Near East, Europe, or the New World. The volume of travel books, new and old, can be gauged from the output of the publisher James Knapton, the fame of Dampier, Rogers, Anson, and other explorers, the success of such editors as John Harris, Thomas Astley, and the Churchill brothers, and the *Term Catalogues* or the reviews of travel books in leading periodicals. Travel books bulk large in the sales catalogues of private libraries, such as those of Defoe, Swift, Adam Smith, Berkeley, Thomson, Goldsmith, Sterne, Walpole, and even Philip Miller, the famous gardener. Dr. Johnson, in his lifelong desire to travel, only expressed a common ambition of his contemporaries when he wrote to Mrs. Piozzi:

> If I had money enough, what would I do?....I might go to Cairo, and down the Red Sea to Bengal, and take a ramble in India. Would this be better than building and planting? It would surely give more variety to the eye, and more amplitude to the mind. Half fourteen thousand would send me out to see other forms of existence, and bring me back to describe them.[12]

Cabin'd, cribb'd, and confin'd at home, he read the travelers. Thomas Gray, as his notebooks and studies show, turned to voyages and travels of all sorts as a "favorite amusement." And William Cowper spoke not for himself alone when he extolled the pleasures of reading the voyagers:

> He travels and expatiates, as the bee
> From flow'r to flow'r, so he from land to land;
> The manners, customs, policy of all
> Pay contribution to the store he gleans;
> He sucks intelligence in ev'ry clime,
> And spreads the honey of his deep research
> At his return—a rich repast for me.
> He travels, and I too. I tread his deck,

[12] *Letters to and from the Late Samuel Johnson, LL.D.*, published by Hester Lynch Piozzi (London, 1788), I, 266.

Ascend his topmast, through his peering eyes
Discover countries, with a kindred heart
Suffer his woes, and share in his escapes;
While fancy, like the finger of a clock,
Runs the great circuit, and is still at home.

The Task, IV, 107–19

It was this age, studious and respectful of the past, astir with new worlds discovered by traveler and explorer, into which Tobias Smollett was born, and in which he sought to make his way as an author and journalist. The influence of travelers and traveling, ancient and contemporary, has been traced extensively in the writings of Swift and Defoe, in poetry, drama, philosophy, aesthetics, and science, yet the understanding of the prose fiction of Tobias Smollett, who traveled more widely and who read more extensively in books of travel than any of his literary contemporaries, has advanced very little beyond Thackeray's oft-repeated observation:

His novels are recollections of his own adventures; his characters drawn, as I should think, from personages with whom he became acquainted in his own career of life. Strange companions he must have had; queer acquaintances he made in the Glasgow college—in the country apothecary's shop; in the gun-room of the man-of-war where he served as a surgeon; and in the hard life on shore, where the sturdy adventurer struggled for fortune. He did not invent much, as I fancy, but had the keenest perceptive faculty, and described what he saw with wonderful relish and delightful broad humor.[13]

Thackeray thus sums up the abiding impression that Smollett has left with readers; yet no one has perceived that Thackeray's criticism can be applied more aptly to a traveler than to a novelist. Captain William Dampier's books, like those of Smollett, are full of recollections of his own adventures, his strange and numerous companions on many ships; he, like Smollett, was a sturdy adventurer who invented little but described what he saw with an accuracy and relish that have made his books a joy to scientists, a mine of rich detail for poets and novelists, and an inspiration to generations of readers. Dampier likewise graced his narrative with a

---

[13] William Makepeace Thackeray, "The English Humourists" (1851), in *The Prose Works*, ed. William Jerrold (London, 1902), pp. 206–7.

vigorous, dignified, expressive style as acceptable in a travel book as Smollett's style is in a novel. Thackeray's words might be applied to other voyagers and travelers whose books are still read, but the comparisons would only further strengthen the impression that a study of Smollett's prose fiction in terms of his varied travel interests and experiences would result in a more discriminating and just appraisal of his novels as literature.

CHAPTER I

SMOLLETT'S FIRST VENTURE BEYOND THE VALLEYS OF THE LEVEN AND THE CLYDE

TO UNDERSTAND Smollett the novelist it is essential to know something about Smollett the traveler. His biography sheds light on his prose fiction, but his prose fiction only confuses and distorts his biography. The personal tone of *Roderick Random*, for example, is so obvious that readers and literary historians have been far too prone to accept the novel as autobiographic in all respects. As a result of hasty identification, accounts of Smollett's early life, his motives for breaking with home ties, his journey up to London, and his participation in the great naval expedition against Carthagena abound in halfhearted conjectures and fancied parallels between Smollett's experiences and those of his hero, Roderick Random. Against such autobiographical comparisons Smollett protested vigorously:

> The only similitude between the circumstances of my own Fortune, and those I have attributed to Roderick Random, consists in my being of a reputable Family in Scotland, in my being bred a Surgeon, and having served as a Surgeon's mate on board of a man of war, during the Expedition to Carthagena. The low situations in which I have exhibited Roderick, I never experienced in my own Person.[1]

This laconic statement, however, can be amplified from sources other than *Roderick Random*.

There is no evidence that he left home because of neglect or a quarrel; throughout life he was on cordial terms with his family and friends in Scotland, and he honored his old master, Dr. Gordon. The motives for his departure are rather

[1] *Letters*, p. 80; cf. pp. 7–8.

to be found in social conditions in Scotland and in Smollett himself. The results of the Union of 1707 were slow in fruition, but in no place were the changes felt so quickly as in Glasgow. As early as the year of Smollett's medical apprenticeship, trade and migration increased rapidly, and it was among the Scots who departed poor from a needy and hard-driven country for the south and the New World that Smollett was swept along by ambition and a spirit of adventure. All his life he restlessly aspired to be affluent and cosmopolitan, and almost certainly as a boy he felt cramped by the limitations of his country. Being the third child of a fourth son, he could expect little assistance from home even if his family had been wealthy, and, doubtless realizing the situation, he set forth while still a lad to make his fortune.

Smollett reached London late in 1739[2] on the eve of a sweeping change in English national life. Walpole, who for nearly twenty years had by various means preserved peace and prosperity for England, now faced formidable opposition in Parliament to which he must yield. A strong popular demand for war against Spain was sweeping the country, but England was both unjustified in pressing the issue and unprepared to prosecute a campaign. War was openly declared on October 19, and sporadic fighting broke out in the Mediterranean and in the West Indies, where Porto Bello was captured on November 22. The formulating of plans and the preparation of an expedition, however, went forward sluggishly, and it was not until July, 1740, that a fleet of approximately twenty-five ships of the line and nine thousand men, exclusive of seamen, were in readiness to sail against the Spanish in the New World. Command was divided among Sir Chaloner Ogle, Admiral Edward Vernon, and Lord Cathcart, who unfortunately died and was succeeded by Brigadier General Wentworth. The expedition after repeated delays sailed from England on October 26.

[2] The only date specified in *Roderick Random* is November 1, 1739, the uniqueness of which suggests that this date may have been chosen because it agreed with that of Smollett's departure for London. See also *Present State of All Nations* (London, 1768), II, 9–10.

Rowlandson

Mutual defiance of Capt: Weazel and Miss Jenny Ramper

One of the largest ships in the fleet was the "Chichester,"[3] a third-rate ship mounting from sixty-four to eighty guns, and normally carrying a complement of over six hundred men, but on this occasion mustering nearly a thousand in all. It was on this great man-of-war that Smollett served as a surgeon's second mate.[4]

Neither Smollett's reasons for joining the expedition nor the circumstances of his assignment to the "Chichester" are known. His career aboard the ship, however, can in part be pieced together from the few logs and musters of his ship that have survived.[5] On the one hand, some impression of what his personal experiences must have been aboard the "Chichester" can be gained from a "Journal" kept by a Lieutenant Robert Watkins from October 1, 1740, to November 1, 1741. Watkins never once mentions Smollett in his rather laconic record, but through the daily entries he unfolds the routine at sea of a great man-of-war. No other record has survived of the Lieutenant, but students of Smollett are most grateful for his "Journal."[6] On the other hand is Smollett's maturer judgment as a historian of these events in his "Account of the Expedition against Carthagena." In a comparison of the animated narrative of *Roderick Random* and the "Journal" and "Account" is to be discerned Smollett's originality and skill as a novelist.

Smollett's naval record is as follows. He received his warrant as a surgeon's second mate on March 10, 1740, and on

3 "Account," *Works*, XII, 191.

4 W. G. P[errin], "Tobias George Smollett," *Mariner's Mirror, the Journal of the Society for Nautical Research*, X (1924), 94, and "Account," *Works*, XII, 191. See also Claude E. Jones, "The British Navy in 1740," *Smollett Studies* (Berkeley and Los Angeles, 1942), pp. 31–40.

5 Public Record Office, Ad. 36/588, 589, and 590. The following records of the "Chichester" were also consulted: Ad. 51/198 (captain's log from September 30, 1740, to January, 1742), Ad. 52/452 (master's log from April 1 to 24, 1740), and Adm. 33/410 (pay book). The abbreviation "P.R.O." will hereafter be used for documents in the Public Record Office in London.

6 P.R.O., Adm. 51/4147. Parts I and II (October 1, 1740, to November 1, 1741) are extant, but Part III (November 1, 1741, to January 23, 1742) is missing. The present study is based on a re-examination of the "Journal" in P.R.O. and later of a photostatic copy kindly lent by Professor Knapp. See also Lewis M. Knapp, "The Naval Scenes in *Roderick Random*," *Publications of the Modern Language Association of America*, XLIX (June, 1934), 593–98.

April 3 he entered the "Chichester" at Blackstakes.[7] Aboard the "Chichester" he found as surgeon John Atkinson, whose warrant dated one week before his own; as surgeon's first mate Robert Jackson Hadsor, and as surgeon's third mate Jacob Taylor, both of whom received their warrants on the same day as Smollett. With one exception he was at all musters from April 3, 1740, until January 30, 1741—that is, approximately from the time the fleet assembled, through the crossing of the Atlantic to the West Indies, until the expedition set sail from Jamaica for Carthagena. While the fleet was gathering below the Downs and at Spithead, Smollett was absent from June 5 through June 30, 1740; on the day he left the ship he borrowed twelve shillings, presumably for a short leave ashore.

The musters from February 1 through April 13, 1741, have disappeared. Within this period falls the most active part of the campaign beginning with the departure of the fleet from Port Royal and including the bulk of the sea and land fighting, the capture of the outer fortifications of Carthagena, and the passage of the fleet into the inner harbor. After this break of two and a half months in the record the musters begin again on April 20, 1741, but on this date Smollett was absent and was not again at musters aboard this ship until June 18. Furthermore, the "Chichester" was back in Port Royal on or shortly before May 20; if Smollett were still absent in part of June, it means that he did not return from Carthagena aboard her. At exactly what date in February, March, or early April, Smollett was transferred or where he was after the "Chichester" was back in port there is no way of determining. It is highly probable, however, that during this period Smollett was in active service elsewhere than on board the "Chichester." Once the expedition reached the West Indies, a shortage of surgeons developed, and the situation was made more acute by an epidemic among the sailors and soldiers before Carthagena. Under such circumstances it is reasonable to assume that Smollett was temporarily

[7] There is no record of his examination; see P.R.O., Ad. 106/2952 and 2963 ("List of Surgeons Examinations").

transferred from the "Chichester." This assumption received some further confirmation from a deathbed statement
made by a surgeon, M'Callum, in 1810 and reported in the
Gentleman's Magazine. Little is known about M'Callum other
than that he spent the early part of his life in naval service
and died at the age of ninety at Queensferry, Scotland, but
in his last moments he was pleased to recall that "at the unsuccessful attack on Carthagena in 1741, he was landed to do
duty as an assistant surgeon to the troops, along with the
celebrated Dr. Smollett, then also an assistant naval surgeon."[8]
The obituary adds that M'Callum "always spoke in terms of
high esteem" of Smollett, which implies that the acquaintance was kept alive through the years.

If this interpretation of the fragmentary records is correct,
it means that during the crucial, most active period of the
expedition Smollett was not aboard the "Chichester." The
significance of this fact will be made apparent later in a discussion of *Roderick Random*.

Smollett was again at musters on the "Chichester" from
June 18 until after the end of August, during which time the
vessel was cleaned and revictualed and returned to England,
where she came to anchor in the Sound on August 31. By
September 21, 1741, the ship was at Tarr Point, but after
this date Smollett no longer was present at weekly musters.[9]

In the pay book on February 17, 1742, the day before the
"Chichester" was placed "in ordinary," Smollett was entered
for gross pay of £42.12.10 and for the following charges:
£2.15.0 for dead men's clothes bought in June and July, 1741,
on the return voyage, £1.1.3 for a chest, and 10s. 8d. for a
comparatively large hospital bill, leaving a balance of
£38.5.11. On May 15, 1742, this sum was paid to James Hen-
shaw, attorney. Among a muster of over a thousand men, the
entry for Smollett is exceptional in not stating that he was
either discharged or transferred. Until further records to the

---

[8] *Gentleman's Magazine*, LXXX (June, 1810), 597.

[9] This is contrary to the statement of the author of the short note in the *Mariner's Mirror* (X, 94) that Smollett remained "in her [the "Chichester"] until she was on 18th February, 1742, transferred to the 'Ordinary' (*i.e.* placed in reserve)."

contrary are discovered, the logical inference is that, shortly after the return of the "Chichester" to England, Smollett left her and was unable to collect his pay in person, either because he was at a distance from the pay office or, as will be suggested later, because he had taken ship again for the West Indies.[10]

Welcome as is this fresh information on Smollett's service during the Carthagena expedition, the story of his years in the West Indies is scarcely less sketchy. It is still necessary to assume, with all his biographers, that Smollett resided for a time in Jamaica; tradition as late as 1873 pointed out the house in Kingston where he lived.[11] He may even have contemplated settling in Jamaica among the many Scots who practically owned and controlled the island.[12] Whatever his sojourn in the West Indies, it was long enough to permit him to meet and court a Creole heiress, Ann Lascelles, who held property near Kingston.[13]

[10] One or two additional facts are to be gained from the musters of the "Chichester." First, Smollett served under four captains: R. Girlington, from April 3 to October 3; Robert Trevor, until his death at Carthagena nearly seven months later on April 18; Stapilton, who brought the ship back into Port Royal and remained on her until June 11; and Osborn, who took over on June 13 and commanded the "Chichester" on the return voyage to England. Second, aboard the "Chichester" during Smollett's service was Lord Elibank, also a Scot, who later at least was known to Smollett. Lord Elibank, in command of Bland's infantry, came on board on October 16, 1740, and was landed at Carthagena on March 19, 1741, with his troops. His "Journal," a copy of which is in the British Museum, is only a very general and impersonal summary of the general course of the expedition. (Add. MS 35898; see especially fol. 33, "Chichester to w.ch I belonged." This statement is confirmed by Watkins' "Journal," March 19, 1741, "A.M. Sent on Shore 30 Soldiers of L: Elebanks and he Went on Shore himself.") Jean Bélanger has called attention to four manuscripts in the British Museum and Public Record Office that should throw further light on Smollett's sources and methods ("Note sur 'Roderick Random' et l'expédition de Carthagène," *Etudes anglaises*, III [juillet-septembre, 1939], 250–51). Among these manuscripts are letters of Captains Stapilton and Osborn. Unfortunately, the war has prevented my examining these documents.

[11] W. J. Gardner, *A History of Jamaica* (London, 1873), p. 128 n.: "Smollett resided in different parts of Jamaica, and for some time in Kingston, where he lodged in a house now occupied as a store in Harbour Street."

[12] R. B. Cunninghame Graham, *Doughty Deeds, an Account of the Life of Robert Graham of Gartmore, Poet & Politician, 1735–1797* (London, 1925). Chapter ii (pp. 13–21, esp. 18–21) affords a fair account of the Scots in Jamaica by one of Smollett's friends—Robert Graham of Gartmore—who went out from Scotland in 1753.

[13] Knapp, "Ann, Wife of Tobias Smollett," *Publications of the Modern Language Association*, XLV (December, 1930), 1033–49.

The assumption that Smollett made a second voyage to the West Indies immediately after his return to England from the Carthagena expedition is supported by a brief statement hitherto overlooked by students of Smollett. In an anonymous "Memoir" of Admiral Charles Knowles published in the *Naval Chronicle* of 1799 occurs the following passage.

As Mr. Smollet was at that time an active writer in support of any party, and treated the account which Admiral Knowles published of the transaction, with much harshness and asperity in the Critical Review, it may be of service to the public, who already have been acquainted with some particulars of Mr. Smollet's history, to know the real motives of this writer's conduct. We state them from undoubted authority, and claim that credit we are confident they deserve.

Dr. Smollet was originally what is termed a loblolly boy, an inferior attendant on the surgeon, on board Commodore Knowles's ship at La Guira. Mr. Knowles gave him his first warrant as surgeon's mate, and in many instances behaved towards him with paternal kindness. Mr. Smollet afterwards published a libel on his patron. The admiral sent and requested to know in what particular he had ever injured him. At length, after much prevarication it appeared, that some favour had been refused him by the admiral's secretary, of which Mr. Knowles was perfectly ignorant. Smollet made his apologies for what had happened, and retired. The worthy admiral, who with surprise beheld the insignificance of the man, who under an apparent zeal for literature, had attacked and sullied the fame of a naval officer, wished and intended to pardon him; *but the Earl of Mansfield, then Mr. Murray, and Hume Campbell, afterwards Lord Register of Scotland, would not suffer it to be done.* Mr. Smollet was therefore prosecuted and fined 100£, was imprisoned a year in Marshalsea, and obliged to find securities for his good behaviour. Mr. Smollet afterwards published a continuation of his History of England, and industriously suppressed, or sedulously distorted, every circumstance that tended to the honour of Admiral Knowles.[14]

This statement, though published some sixty years after the event referred to, appears at least to have a limited foundation in fact. First of all, the editor of the *Naval Chronicle* in 1799 was John Jones, a member of a Welsh family who for four generations were publishers, editors, and

---

[14] *Naval Chronicle*, I (1799), 120–21. The term "loblolly boy" applied by the sailors to Roderick (*Roderick Random*, II, 51) and to Smollett in the above passage was in both instances obviously used as a term of contempt. The *NED* records as variants "loblolly man" and "loblolly doctor." As applied to Roderick and Smollett it meant simply a servant or mate to a surgeon, or even the surgeon himself ([Captain Francis Grose], *A Classical Dictionary of the Vulgar Tongue* [London, 1785], p. 104).

bibliophiles. John Jones himself was during many years editor of the *Naval Chronicle* and the *European Magazine* and was in turn the father of John Winter Jones, principal librarian of the British Museum. His brother was Stephen Jones, editor of Baker's *Biographia dramatica*, and his father was Giles Jones, author of children's books and collaborator with Griffith Jones, his more famous brother, who, according to John Nichols,[15] was associated with Goldsmith and Smollett in the *British Magazine* and with Johnson in the *Literary Magazine*. The Joneses were just such a family as can be trusted on matters of literary history. If John Jones did not write the "Memoir," he certainly approved of it and may have himself supplied information on Smollett that came down to him from his great-uncle.[16]

In the second place, throughout the "Memoir" as a whole the author was exceptionally scrupulous for his age in citing sources in private letters, memorials, naval records, as well as standard published works. In fact, modern naval historians often rank the "Memoir" among primary sources.[17] It may be added that a comparison of the standard biographies of Knowles, Campbell, and Mansfield with the "Memoir" reveals no disagreement in statement of facts.

Finally, the passage confirms rather than contradicts what already was known of Smollett's relations with Knowles. To appreciate the full import of the revelations here made it is necessary to glance ahead some twenty-five years. In 1758 Knowles defended his seamanship in a pamphlet entitled *The Conduct of Admiral Knowles on the Late Expedition Set in a True Light*, which was very sharply criticized by Smollett in the *Critical Review*.[18] Knowles was highly offended and instituted a suit for libel leading to Smollett's conviction. It was in relation to this affair that the above-quoted statement was

---

[15] *Literary Anecdotes* (London, 1812), III, 465–66.

[16] For this suggestion I am indebted to Professor Knapp.

[17] G. E. Mánwaring, *A Bibliography of British Naval History* (London, 1930), p. 52; Admiral Herbert William Richmond, *The Navy in the War of 1739–1748* (Cambridge, 1920), I, 117, 251; and Sir John Knox Laughton, "Knowles," *DNB*.

[18] *Critical Review*, V (May, 1758), 438–39.

made in the "Memoir." Although the passage in question clears up much that was formerly obscure in Smollett's relation with Knowles and Campbell, there is no occasion at present to go into the ramifications of the lawsuit.[19]

Accepting the first part of the statement that Smollett served under Knowles at La Guaira, the train of events may have proceeded as follows. Shortly after leaving the "Chichester" at Tarr Point, England, in September, 1741, Smollett obtained a commission in a merchant ship that sailed almost immediately, and later in the West Indies he approached Knowles for a commission. Or there is the possibility that Smollett had his commission from Knowles before he sailed from England. From the captain's logs[20] it appears that Knowles received his commission on September 5, 1742, his order for the expedition against La Guaira on October 14, and that he sailed on November 12 in command of the "Suffolk," accompanied by the "Burford" and the "Comet"; and that later at Antigua he was joined by the "Assistance," the "Advice," the "Norwich," the "Eltham," the "Lively," and the "Scarborough." The expedition attacked La Guaira unsuccessfully on February 19–20, 1743, and was back in England at Spithead on August 7 of the same year.[21]

[19] Alice Parker, "Tobias Smollett and the Law," *Studies in Philology*, XXXIX (July, 1942), 545–58; Knapp, "Rex versus Smollett: More Data on the Smollett-Knowles Libel Case," *Modern Philology*, XLI (May, 1944), 221–27. The evidence shows that Smollett served only three months, was fined £100, and was confined not in Marshalsea but King's Bench Prison (Harold Stein, "Smollett's Imprisonment," *Times Literary Supplement*, May 5, 1927, p. 318). The "Memoir" is perhaps also incorrect in asserting that Knowles gave Smollett his first commission.

It is to be remembered that Campbell's antagonism to Smollett dated back at least to 1753, when Peter Gordon retained Campbell as counsel who prosecuted a suit of assault against Smollett with unmistakable personal animosity (*Letters*, pp. 15–23, 57, 58, 62, 130–31; H. P. Vincent, "Tobias Smollett's Assault on Gordon and Groom," *Review of English Studies*, XVI [April, 1940], 183–88). As for Knowles, it is quite possible that Smollett approached him for a favor. Knowles was governor of Jamaica from 1752 to 1756, during the period when Smollett was having considerable difficulty with his Jamaica holdings and may have asked his assistance. Later Knowles may have hit upon this request as an excuse in his efforts to compromise the libel suit.

[20] P.R.O., Adm. 51/944.

[21] This chronology agrees with the one adduced by Buck from the story of Melopoyn in *Peregrine Pickle* (Howard S. Buck, *A Study in Smollett* [New Haven, 1925], pp. 57–62).

There are two objections to the conclusion that Smollett served in the La Guaira expedition under Knowles. First, Smollett does not allude to it in his letters, and his only reference to it elsewhere is a sentence in his *History* in which he asserts that "the commodore [Knowles] abandoned the enterprize . . . . without having added much to his reputation either as to conduct or resolution."[22] It is true that Smollett was silent on a great many important events in his life, yet it is hard to understand how, without some association with Knowles other than the very impersonal contacts of the Carthagena expedition, he was prompted to write of the Admiral:

> Ask his character of those who know him, they will not scruple to say, he is an admiral without conduct, an engineer without knowledge, an officer without resolution, and a man without veracity. They will tell you he is an ignorant, assuming, officious, fribbling pretender; conceited as a peacock, obstinate as a mule, and mischievous as a monkey; that in every station of life he has played the tyrant with his inferiors, the incendiary among his equals, and commanded a sq——n occasionally for twenty years, without having even established his reputation in the article of personal courage.[23]

The second objection—and this at first sight would seem to carry more weight than the first—is that Smollett's name is not entered in the muster roll or the pay book of the "Suffolk" covering the La Guaira expedition,[24] nor does it appear in the extant muster rolls of any of the other ships. There remains, then, always the possibility that Smollett served a second time in the British navy and that on the second occasion he had his commission from Knowles and participated in the disastrous attack on La Guaira. Whatever his adventures and sojourn in the West Indies were, Smollett was settled in London by May 22, 1744. On this date he wrote: "I have moved into the house where the late John Douglas, surgeon, died, and you may henceforth direct for Mr. Smollett, surgeon, in Downing Street, West."

The fragmentary records of Smollett's journey up to Lon-

---

[22] *A Complete History of England* (London, 1760), XI, 160.

[23] *Critical Review*, V, 438–39.

[24] P.R.O., Adm. 36/402 and 403 and Ad. 33/381.

don, his voyages in the British navy, and his sojourn in the West Indies afford no insight into what these experiences meant in terms of Smollett's personality and memory. Naval histories, such as those of Hannay or Richmond, can give some meaning to the dry bones of dates and places and names but nothing specific about Smollett. It takes no great imagination, however, to realize that adventuring up to London, serving in a great naval expedition, and visiting and perhaps residing in the West Indies brought to the young Scotsman Smollett a wealth of memorable, if not extraordinary, experiences. Even so, it is doubtful if the record would be worth reading were it not that he responded more intensely than others and, in Thackeray's words, "described what he saw with wonderful relish and delightful broad humour."

CHAPTER II

A SCOTTISH SURGEON'S SECOND MATE
IN THE ROYAL NAVY

THE vivid memories of Carthagena and perhaps of La Guaira, of the perilous and strange lives of seamen, remained with Smollett long after he left the navy, and to these memories he returned later in his prose fiction. When he settled in Downing Street, London, in 1744, however, he did not aspire to write novels but to practice medicine. Only when time passed and the lucrative practice did not materialize did he gradually resort to writing for a living. First he revised his youthful tragedy, *The Regicide*, which was in his pocket when he went up to London in 1739, but the producers would have nothing to do with it. He next tried his hand at two satiric poems, *Advice* (1746) and *Reproof* (1747), without much success. Sometime before May, 1744, according to his own account, he went abroad to improve himself "by travelling, in France and other foreign countries."[1] The knowledge of the French language and literature he thereby gained he turned to account in translating Le Sage's *Gil Blas*, which was published in October, 1748. On November of the same year he announced a projected translation of *Don Quixote*; sometime prior to this date he apparently spent six weeks abroad to study Spanish "amongst the native Spaniards, at Brussels."[2] It was in 1747, concurrently with these other literary undertakings, that Smollett

[1] *Letters*, p. 80.

[2] [John Shebbeare], *The Occasional Critic* (London, 1756), p. 61 n. For a favorable estimate of Shebbeare's reliability see James R. Foster, "Smollett's Pamphleteering Foe Shebbeare," *Publications of the Modern Language Association*, LVII (December, 1942), 1053–1100.

wrote in eight months his first novel, *Roderick Random*, and published it in January, 1748.[3] As a result of his travels abroad, his residence in London, and his widening acquaintance with English and European literature, Smollett brought to the novel not only his memories but also considerable literary maturity and critical perception. *Roderick Random* is by no means the work of a novice; the excellent critical Preface should be enough to refute any such conception. In view of his knowledge and experience, it is not surprising that, in recounting the unlooked-for, obscure, harrowing experiences of a young Scottish surgeon, Smollett produced a book fashioned after established literary models. To trace the metamorphosis of raw experience into literary fiction is the purpose of the following pages.

The first sailor that Smollett introduces in *Roderick Random* is Roderick's maternal uncle, Captain Bowling, who rescues Rory from the neglect of his guardian grandfather and helps him to settle a long score with a tyrannizing schoolmaster. Captain Bowling apprentices Roderick to an apothecary and then goes to sea as lieutenant aboard the "Thunder." He soon quarrels with his commander, Captain Oakum, and after a duel at Tiburon Bay, Hispaniola, in which he leaves his captain for dead, he escapes to France to serve in the navy. In the meantime Roderick, who has come up to London, is impressed aboard the "Thunder," incurs Oakum's malice, and is chained to the deck. While he lies in this predicament, the "Thunder," with several other ships, participates in a brush with a squadron of French warships, aboard one of which, by coincidence, Bowling is serving as quartermaster. Later Bowling, while on a pirating cruise, learns that Oakum has survived his wound, whereupon he returns to England, fits out a ship, and sails with Roderick in the slave trade. During the voyage from Deal to Guinea, he meets a vessel which appears to be a French man-of-war. He thereupon delivers a harangue in Morgan's best vein to arouse his men to the attack, but the ship turns out to be English.

[3] Knapp, "Smollett's Early Years in London," *Journal of English and Germanic Philology*, XXXI (April, 1932), 220-27.

After six months of trafficking along the coast of Angola and Benguela, where they collect some four hundred slaves, Bowling and Roderick depart for South America, whence, once the cargo has been sold and incidentally Roderick discovers his long-lost father, Captain Bowling directs his course to England, there to end a successful voyage.

No trace of the original of Captain Bowling is to be found in Smollett's experiences in the navy; save for the humors of the Captain's salty idiom, his origins are purely literary. The plan, many of the incidents, and the point of view of the narrative are reminiscent of the sea tradition found even in the Greek and later French heroic-romances. Heliodorus' and Gomberville's, like Smollett's, tales are told from the point of view of the officers rather than of the common seamen and abound in shipwrecks, plunderings, treachery, quarrels, revenge, and fortuitous coincidence. In the late seventeenth and early eighteenth centuries the same tradition flourished in the many books produced by the buccaneers and privateers. Esquemeling, Sharpe, Ringrose, Wafer, Dampier, Rogers, and Shelvocke in their books concentrated on plot and counterplot, battles, escapes, shipwrecks, scenes of dire distress, and drunken profligacy; and, although piracy began to die out around 1700, the tradition of sea life fostered by these men continued to dominate for fifty years English ships and the books written by English seamen. In his own day Smollett had an excellent example of adventurous sea life in Anson's expedition, which sailed from England in 1740 and after many extraordinary adventures returned to England in June, 1744. The several books by Bulkeley and Cummins, Campbell, and Anson that grew out of this expedition recount almost every violent experience that men can have at sea.

Smollett had more immediate models for Captain Bowling and his career in the prose fiction written in imitation of the buccaneers and pirates. Swift, Defoe, Chetwood, and others owed some of their immediate success and much of their material to the voyagers, but they still conformed to the traditional pattern of the heroic-romance. Their foremost characters are Captains Gulliver, Singleton, Avery, Boyle, and

Rowlandson

Rod: Random discovers his Uncle Bowling in distress

Falconer, and the staple of their stories is the extraordinary adventure and the daring exploration.[4] Smollett in no way distinguishes Captain Bowling from Defoe's sea adventurers, the privateers, or the captains of the Greek romances, and, as a step in the development of the prose fiction of the sea, Captain Bowling and his career are negligible.

Elsewhere in *Roderick Random*, in episodes that do not involve Captain Bowling, are easily recognized traces of the traditional heroic-romance of sea adventure. The most notable example is Roderick's shipwreck on the Sussex coast, the details for which Smollett took directly from the wreck of one of Anson's boats, the "Wager," on the coast of what is now Chile.[5] Smollett doubtless included the incident to capitalize on the stir over the various fortunes of the men who had recently returned from Anson's expedition. The wreck of the "Wager," however, owes its later fame to Captain John Byron, "Foul-weather Jack," who at the time was only a midshipman aboard her but whose *Narrative* (1768) supplied his more famous grandson Lord Byron with firsthand material for the shipwreck in *Don Juan*.

The story of the "Wager," according to Bulkeley and Cummins' version as told in their *Voyage to the South Seas 1740–1741* (1743), is as follows. On the voyage out from England, Captain Kidd, originally of the "Wager," died aboard the "Pearl" and was succeeded by Captain Murray, then in command of the "Wager." Cheap, as yet only a first mate, succeeded Murray in command of the "Wager." Off the Chilean coast near the Gulf de la Penas, against the advice of the gunner Bulkeley, Captain Cheap ran the ship aground, whereupon he went ashore in the first landing party, leaving some of the crew to rifle the ship and get drunk. When the boatswain came ashore, Cheap knocked him down and later in haste shot Cozens, a midshipman. Eventually the crew split up into two parties and returned to England by different routes.

[4] Harold Francis Watson, *The Sailor in English Fiction and Drama* (New York, 1931), chap. ii, "The Sailor in the Voyage Narratives."

[5] Attention was first called to the parallel by Professor Watson in *The Sailor in English Fiction*, pp. 166–68.

Turning now to *Roderick Random*, it will be recalled that, subsequent to the attack on Carthagena and a brief shore duty in the West Indies, Roderick returns to England aboard the "Lizard." On the homeward passage the captain dies, and the first mate, Crampley, formerly of the "Thunder," takes command. Just as Cheap made Cozens a scapegoat, so Crampley persecutes Tomlins until he commits suicide. Ignoring the warning of the gunner, Crampley sets the course of the ship landward and eventually wrecks her on the Sussex coast. He hastens ashore in the first boatload, leaving the ship in the hands of a pillaging and drunken crew. Roderick forces his way into the boat with Crampley, and, once ashore, he and Crampley engage in a duel, the outcome of which is that Roderick is treacherously struck down from the rear and left for dead. Several less striking parallels are given by Watson, including what may be merely an accidental similarity between Bulkeley and Crampley and Cummins and Tomlins.

To say that Smollett took the incident from Bulkeley and Cummins' book is, however, to ignore the fact that Smollett had a number of opportunities to hear the story from several of the participants in the disaster. The evidence is supplied by Alexander Carlyle in his *Autobiography*.[6] As a young man in London in 1746, fresh from his medical studies in Leiden, Carlyle went to the British Coffee-House and there found many of his old friends from Scotland, was introduced to Smollett, with whom he often associated, and met Captain Cheap recently returned from the wreck of the "Wager" on the Chilean coast. While in the coffee-house, Cheap regaled the company with his experiences, which were of great interest to Carlyle. It is hard to believe that Smollett, who also frequented the British Coffee-House, as will be pointed out later, did not hear of the wreck of the "Wager" from Cheap's own lips.[7]

---

[6] Alexander Carlyle, *Autobiography* (Edinburgh and London, 1860), pp. 191–94.

[7] Smollett later enjoyed the friendship of at least one member of the expedition, Captain Robert Mann, who, unlike Cheap, had sailed around the globe with Anson. Their acquaintance may have begun as early as 1746 or 1747 in the London coffee-

Smollett concentrated his attention, however, not on other voyagers or expeditions, but upon the Carthagena expedition in which he himself had participated. Contemporary interest in the course and outcome of the expedition was out of all proportion to the strategic or political consequences, even had the expedition succeeded in all its objectives. With a desire to fix the responsibility for the failure and to punish the delinquents, the English public turned to the navy itself and to the conduct of the commanders of both branches of the service. Admiral Vernon, a man of political aspirations, had an itch for the pen, and he undertook to defend himself and attack others in a long series of pamphlets. Sooner or later almost every rank in the army and navy was heard from, and the press was full of reports. It was in this drawn-out controversy that Smollett wrote first *Roderick Random* in 1747, and fifteen years after the events he prepared a balanced, impersonal, historical version in his "Account of the Expedition against Carthagena," which he published in his *Compendium of Authentic and Entertaining Voyages* in 1756.[8] This is not the occasion to discuss the merits of Smollett's contribution to the controversy but to discover with what skill he transformed experience and knowledge into fiction.

Roderick was pressed into service, and, though Smollett escaped this violence, hundreds of other men were seized to man the ships for the Carthagena expedition. Seldom has the British navy been reduced to such desperate means of raising a fleet. Parliament and the press resounded with debates, and the bounty for an able seaman went up to two guineas. Just how many men were impressed for the "Chichester" is not known.[9] Watkins' only references to the subject were on January 21, 24, and 25, 1741, when he mentions receiving on board in Port Royal thirty-two impressed men; but all who have looked into the subject have found *Roderick*

---

houses, when Anson had returned in triumph (*Letters*, p. 46; cf. *Humphry Clinker*, II, 96).

[8] "Account," *Works*, XII, 192.

[9] Watkins came aboard six months to a day after Smollett and when the lists were pretty much made up.

Random an undistorted and strictly authentic recital of the tactics of a press-gang.[10]

The first entries in Watkins' "Journal" that have a bearing on *Roderick Random* record in full a storm encountered by the fleet shortly after leaving England. Even a landsman can sense in the allusions to reefings and torn sails the violence of the gale and the feverish activity aboard the "Chichester." Watkins speaks of the "Buckingham" losing her main mast and of the distress of the fleet as a whole and, on a later occasion, mentions in passing: "Lost two men over board off the Maine Yard & was Drown'd." Smollett in his "Account" includes these details and adds that, at the same time the two men were lost from the main yards, a third had his knee "crushed in a terrible manner between the beril and the mast."[11] All these incidents are mentioned in *Roderick Random*, and from the injuring of the sailor's knee, too insignificant to be noticed by Watkins, Smollett has constructed one of the great episodes of the novel—the quarrel between the Drs. Mackshane, Thomson, and Random over Jack Rattlin's broken leg, and the courage with which the honest tar faces the prospects of an amputation.[12]

On January 7, 1741, a few days before the fleet entered Port Royal, Watkins has the following entry:

at 6 AM. Saw 5 Saile Under Hispaniola ye Admir! made ye Signal for ye fleet to Tack all the Fleet Tackt ye E wd: at 9 a Signal for Six Ships to Chace.

The next allusion to this incident comes on January 10, when the fleet was anchored in Port Royal:

at 5 Anchord here yᵉ Ships as we Left in Chace off Hispaniola Viz. Prince Frederick, Orford, Augusta, Dunkirk, York, and Weymouth; I find these Ships have bin Engaged with those Ships We Saw they began in

[10] Richmond, *The Navy in the War of 1739–1748*, Vol. I, Appendix III, "The Marines and the Manning Question"; J. R. Hutchinson, *The Press-Gang Afloat and Ashore* (New York, 1914); Robert Beatson, *Naval and Military Memoirs of Great Britain* (London, 1804), I, 53–55; Smollett, *History of England*, XI, 66–68; R. Pares, "The Manning of the Navy in the West Indies, 1702–63," *Transactions of the Royal Historical Society*, XX (4th ser., 1937), 31–60; and Dora Mae Clark, "The Impressment of Seamen in the American Colonies," *Essays in Colonial History Presented to Charles McLean Andrews by His Students* (New Haven, 1931), pp. 198–224.

[11] "Account," *Works*, XII, 192.   [12] *Roderick Random*, II, 63–66.

the night Taking them for Spanish Ships but in the morning found them to be french Ships. The Orford & some others of our Ships have Receiv'd Damage and I find by Accounts We have lost Several men And Several much Wounded.

A fuller description of the fight is given in a letter by Sam Speed to the Duke of Newcastle, principal secretary of state, and in a French letter, apparently by the Vicomte de Roquefeuil.[13] With these reports Smollett in the "Account" is in full accord, save that he singles out the "Orford," instead of the "Prince Frederick," as the first ship to engage the French fleet and the ship upon which the captain of the marines had his head blown off.

In *Roderick Random* the engagement between the British and the French is described in the following language:

> It was almost dark when we came up with the sternmost chase, which we hailed, and inquired who they were: they gave us to understand they were French men-of-war; upon which Captain Oakum commanded them to send their boat on board of him; but they refused, telling him, if he had any business with them, to come on board of their ship: he then threatened to pour in a broadside upon them, which they promised to return. Both sides were as good as their word; and the engagement began with great fury. . . . . I concealed my agitation as well as I could, till the head of the officer of the marines, who stood near me, being shot off, bounced from the deck athwart my face. . . . .
>
> The engagement lasted till broad day, when Captain Oakum, finding that he was like to gain neither honour nor advantage by the affair, pretended to be undeceived by seeing their colours; and hailing the ship with whom he had fought all night, protested he believed them Spaniards, and the guns being silenced on each side, ordered the barge to be hoisted out, and went on board the French commodore. Our loss amounted to ten killed, and eighteen wounded, most part of whom afterwards died.[14]

From a comparison between this passage and the several reports of the engagement, it is clear that Smollett in one inci-

---

[13] *Report on the Manuscripts of the Duke of Buccleuch and Queensbury, K.G., K.T., Preserved at Montagu House, Whitehall* (Historical Manuscripts Commission, London, 1899), I, 394–96. For two other independent accounts which agree with Speed see Beatson, *Naval and Military Memoirs*, I, 69–70, which appears to have been taken from Knowles' journal, and G. Lacour-Gayet, *La Marine militaire de la France sous le règne de Louis XV* (Paris, 1910), pp. 140–42. The latter is apparently drawn from a letter of Vicomte de Roquefeuil published in *Carnet historique et litteraire*, III (1899), 109–13, of which I have been unable to consult a copy.

[14] *Roderick Random*, II, 68–70; Smollett later repeats this in the same details in the "Account" (*Works*, XII, 195).

dent of the novel no longer followed the fortunes of his own
ship but shifted the scene of action from the "Chichester" to
the "Prince Frederick."

A second parallel between the account of the engagement
of the "Thunder" before Carthagena and that of the "Prince
Frederick" suggests that Smollett may have served for a
while aboard the latter vessel. Of the six ships sent to over-
take the French, only the "Prince Frederick" took part in
the futile and nerve-wracking attack on the forts of Boca
Chica.[15] In fact, Watkins' "Journal" offers no evidence what-
soever that the "Chichester" ever fired a gun, except as a
salute, or that she ever lost a man in a battle. It is apparent,
rather, that the "Chichester" acted almost exclusively in an
auxiliary capacity to both the military forces and the navy,
sending boats and men frequently to land troops, artillery,
and supplies and lending equipment to other ships. For example, from April 8 to 17, 1741, the "Chichester" partially
outfitted and manned with fourteen of her crew the captured
Spanish ship "Gallicia"; on April 30 she sent a midshipman
and twenty men aboard the "Prince Frederick" and earlier,
on March 24, two lieutenants, forty-six seamen, twelve
soldiers, and a lieutenant aboard the "Weymouth." In view
of all the evidence, it is probable that, if Smollett ever was involved in active fighting, he was either ashore on hospital
duty or aboard another ship to which he was temporarily
transferred. As has already been remarked, Smollett was absent from muster on the "Chichester" from April 20 through
June 11 and perhaps also in February and March—a fact
which supports this assumption. To follow his movements,
however, during the time the fleet was before Carthagena is
practically impossible. His name is not on the books of the
"Prince Fredrick,"[16] but, even if he had sailed aboard her for
a short period, he doubtless would not be entered on her
records.[17] All that can be concluded is this: though the Boca

[15] The other ships were the "Boyne," the "Hampton Court," the "Tilbury," and
the "Suffolk."

[16] P.R.O., Adm. 36/2540 and 2541 (muster).

[17] In the many musters of the Carthagena expedition I examined, I found no
instance of a temporary transfer being recorded. What was the customary practice
in the navy in 1740 I do not know.

Chica attack was as ill advised and futile as the pursuit of the French squadron had been and though it was accorded more extensive notices than the former in the many reports on the expedition, it was not the major maneuver; but Smollett, shifting the scene of action the second time from the "Chichester" to the "Prince Frederick," expanded the Boca Chica engagement into his longest naval scene, with a full description of the fierce cannonading as experienced from below deck in the surgeon's quarters.

Instances might be multiplied to show how again and again Smollett selected secondary events, not necessarily autobiographic, and made them the basis for realistic pictures of daily life aboard a man-of-war. In one place he makes the hero of *Roderick Random* observe:

Instead of small beer, each man was allowed three half-quarterns of brandy or rum, which was distributed every morning, diluted with a certain quantity of his water, without either sugar or fruit to render it palatable; for which reason, this composition was, by the sailors, not unaptly styled *Necessity*.[18]

Watkins records that on several occasions he served brandy and water to the crew of the "Chichester." This mixture is almost certainly what is now called grog, so named after Admiral Vernon, who was known as "Old Grog" from the grogram cloth cloak he wore and who in August, 1740, gave the first order that such a drink should be served in the navy.[19] Roderick's almost fatal illness reflects in part Smollett's own illness, though unrecorded in the musters yet attested by a rather large hospital bill of 10s. 8d. in the pay book of the "Chichester," but Roderick's illness also reflects the epidemic raging on every hand. While the "Chichester" was before Carthagena, Watkins made almost daily entries of deaths by fever among the crew, and he often transferred sick crew members to hospital ships or sent them ashore to hospitals in Port Royal. Roderick complains of the mess, and Watkins frequently speaks of condemning spoiled food. Yet, somewhat surprisingly, Watkins' "Journal" recounts a num-

[18] *Roderick Random*, II, 93–94.

[19] Admiral Vernon also lent his name to the great shrine of American independence—Mount Vernon—through Lawrence Washington, who was in the Carthagena expedition.

ber of conspicuous events that are not mentioned by Smollett. Among these are the death of several officers, the selling before the mast of dead men's clothes (of which Smollett bought some on the return voyage), the many floggings, the mutiny of the soldiers, and the running the gauntlet by men caught stealing. Where was Smollett when, as Watkins reports, "Samuel Murray was Whipt for Mutiny, because y[e] Stewart would not give him his meat raw"?[20]

The excellence of *Roderick Random* lies not in the episodes but in the characters, and here Watkins and all other records of the "Chichester" give no help; in truth it is unsafe to look for any. There is nothing in Watkins, in the logs, the pay books, the muster of the "Chichester," or in any record of the Carthagena expedition that warrants identifying any of Roderick's companions with an actual person.[21] This applies with special force to the character of Captain Oakum. Everyone who studies Smollett is sooner or later subjectively convinced that, in Oakum, Smollett described Admiral (then Captain) Knowles. There is a great temptation to see in the close association of the "Chichester" with the "Weymouth," commanded by Knowles and often spoken of by Watkins, an opportunity for Smollett to have observed and even met Knowles. There is also the curious digression when Roderick, on the return of the fleet to Port Royal, was transferred to the "Lizard" for patrol duty and later sailed in her to England. One may be tempted to suspect that Smollett here had in mind a patrol sent out by Admiral Vernon in June, 1741, to watch the Spanish and protect trade and guard the approaches to Jamaica. During this maneuver Knowles commanded the "Litchfield" and Davers the "Suffolk," and, from all that can be learned of their movements, this particular patrol is the only one carried out by British boats during the summer of 1741 that bears any resemblance to the cruise

[20] "Journal," December 18, 1740.

[21] Chambers (*Smollett*, p. 40) suggested that Captain "Whiffle images . . . . Lord Harry Pawlett, commander of the *Harfleur*, who died in 1794, the last Duke of Bolton," but offered no evidence for his conclusion.

of the "Lizard."[22] Smollett, however, is not entered in the rolls of the "Litchfield" or the "Suffolk,"[23] and the musters of the "Chichester" place him aboard that ship during the time the "Litchfield" cruised around the West Indies and returned to England. If Oakum is Knowles, the portrait was not drawn from personal relations during the Carthegana expedition or the summer after; and if one insists on seeing a personal bias in the portrayal of a character, it is necessary to look to an association between Smollett and Knowles during the La Guaira expedition, and of this there is only a probability. In the long run, it is wiser to regard the characters, like the incidents, as founded, not upon particular personal experiences, but upon Smollett's wide observation during his service in the British navy. Only then can the student and critic escape the autobiographical bias that has colored far too much of the criticism of Smollett and his novels.

If the historical prototypes of Smollett's characters are unknown, his literary models are not far to seek. Just as Shakespeare, in the underplot of *Henry V*, brought together in an interplay of racial loyalties Fluellen the Welshman, Macmorris the Irishman, Jamy the Scotsman, and Pistol the Englishman, so Smollett in *Roderick Random* assembled on board the "Thunder" a motley collection of sailors of various nationalities. Here, as in the play, much of the action arises from the conflict of the racial antipathies of Captain Oakum and Crampley, the Englishmen; Dr. Mackshane, the Irish surgeon; Dr. Morgan, the Welshman; and Roderick, the Scot, with similar affectionate partiality for the loyalty of the Welsh and scorn for the false pride of the English. Further, Smollett's Morgan is directly descended from Fluellen in disposition, in character, and in manner of speech. Beyond question Smollett consciously imitated the humors of Jonson, Shakespeare, and Shadwell in the delineation of many more characters which he drew from those parts of life "where the

[22] E[dward] V[ernon], *Original Papers Relating to the Expedition to Carthagena* (London, 1744), p. 147; Beatson, *Naval and Military Memoirs*, p. 111; *Naval Chronicle*, I, 100; and *DNB*, LVIII, 271.

[23] P.R.O., Adm. 51/521 (log); Adm. 36/1768 (muster); and Adm. 51/943 (muster of "Suffolk," September 4–October 26, 1741).

humours and passions are undisguised by affectation, cere-
mony, or education; and the whimsical peculiarities of disposition appear as nature has implanted them."[24]

His professed models were, however, Cervantes, Le Sage,
and picaresque novels in which travel and fiction were often
blended. Like Cervantes, he intended ultimately to convert
"romance to purposes far more useful and entertaining, by
making it assume the sock and point out the follies of ordinary life. The same method," he continued, "has been prac-
tised by other Spanish and French authors, and by none
more successfully than by Monsieur Le Sage, who, in his *Adventures of Gil Blas*, has described the knavery and foibles of
life, with infinite humour and sagacity." Unlike Le Sage, who
in Smollett's opinion made Gil Blas the butt of the satire,
Smollett wished to awaken compassion for his hero, to which
end he endowed him with a good birth, an education, and
"modest merit." These several conditions were to be naturally fulfilled by "making the chief personage of this work a
North Briton," for, Smollett explains,

I could at a small expense bestow on him such education as I thought the
dignity of his birth and character required, which could not possibly be
obtained in England, by such slender means as the nature of my plan would
afford. In the next place, I could represent simplicity of manners in a
remote part of the kingdom, with more propriety than in any other place
near the capital; and, lastly, the disposition of the Scots, addicted to
travelling, justifies my conduct in deriving an adventurer from that
country.[25]

Appropriately enough the hero is christened "Roderick" for
his Scottish origins and is named "Random" for his aimless
peregrinations. At Roderick's birth his mother dreams of having conceived a tennis ball, which, acccording to a Highland
seer, portended that the offspring "would be a great traveller."

Elsewhere in the Preface to *Roderick Random*, Smollett
goes on to say: "I have attempted to represent modest merit
struggling with every difficulty to which a friendless orphan
is exposed, from his own want of experience, as well as from
the selfishness, envy, malice, and base indifference of man-

[24] *Roderick Random*, I, xlii.   [25] *Ibid*.

kind."[26] In this part of his plan Smollett paralleled Vincente Espinel, another picaresque writer mentioned earlier, who wrote his autobiographic *Vida de Marcos de Obregón* "to show in his misfortunes and adversities how poor esquires may overcome the difficulties of the world and breast the perils of time and fortune."[27] Smollett likewise followed the precedent of Le Sage and Cervantes in choosing low scenes, vulgar adventures of the fabliau order, but more especially in developing the antiheroic or antiromantic tone, exposing false pride and hypocrisy, and "unmasking the sordid disposition of the world." Each of the three novels—*Don Quixote*, *Gil Blas*, and *Roderick Random*—consists of a succession of loosely linked episodes: Don Quixote wanders far afield in a checkered quest; with each new master, Gil Blas comes in contact with a different class or profession; and Roderick Random, as he roves about at home and abroad, encounters many nationalities and is forced to make many adjustments to strange environments. That Smollett frequently approximated the style and plan of Le Sage is not surprising when it is remembered that he translated *Gil Blas* and prepared a critical essay on picaresque fiction concurrently with the composition of *Roderick Random*.

Smollett's choice and handling of the naval episodes in *Roderick Random* may be accounted for in part by the example of picaresque fiction; yet Roderick is not strictly a picaro, and there is nothing antiheroic about Morgan, Rattlin, or Oakum. Smollett was impressed too deeply by the incompetence, oppression, and tragedy which he saw around him not to swerve occasionally from the genial temper of the comic spirit to the sardonic smile of the satirist. Too often to the disadvantage of his novels, however, he was a satirist by temperament and not by knowledge or precept.

In general, Smollett interpreted his experiences more like a traveler than a biographer or a historian. He subordinated a survey of a campaign in order to relate the circumscribed ex-

[26] *Ibid.*, pp. xli–xlii.

[27] *Vida de Marcos de Obregón* (Madrid, 1922), I, 43, "Relación primera de la vida del escudero Marcos de Obregón."

periences of a surgeon's second mate who is more of a spectator than a protagonist. Roderick is pressed into service,
wins tolerance by his humanity and his fists, makes friends and
enemies, attends the sick and wounded, survives a fierce engagement, suffers from the epidemical fevers—all with the
ultimate realization that he is but undergoing the normal
routine of a seaman's life. He is unaware of the councils of
captains, the deeds of the titled, or the exploits of the heroic,
and, as far as he is concerned, one naval expedition is much
like another. In a sense he never loses the landlubber's outlook; he is never completely at home at sea. As a result, compared with historical narratives, *Roderick Random* is fragmentary, unbalanced, and limited in outlook, but it has the
convincing quality of an eyewitness account.

If there is any guiding principle of organization back of the
story of the Carthagena expedition in *Roderick Random*, it
would seem to be this: in the novel Smollett was content to
narrate his minor role in the campaign, to describe conditions
as they touched him or came to his attention, and, selecting
an anecdote here and there, to illustrate the hard life of his
companions. The emphasis is on men and manners, and yet,
incomplete as it is, *Roderick Random* remains the best-known
version of the Carthagena expedition:

> He [Smollett] helped to make his generation understand what a hate-
> fully cruel thing military inefficiency is, and how surely the wretched per-
> sonal squabbles of leaders mean death and useless suffering to the men
> who are so unhappy as to be placed at their mercy. It is, I hope, not very
> ferocious to think with some complacency that Smollett unwittingly, but
> not the less beneficially, helped to prepare the people of England to insist
> on the execution of Admiral Byng, and to give all leaders in war an un-
> forgetable warning that their personal feelings were not to come in the
> way of the discharge of their duty. Even if he did not influence the mind
> of his generation in this way, he did a considerable feat when he gave the
> best literary picture of a military expedition left by an eye-witness in the
> eighteenth century. Carlyle . . . . has declared that almost the only no-
> ticeable feature in the whole expedition was the presence of Tobias
> Smollett. This much at least is certain, that without Tobias Smollett the
> Carthagena expedition would be a much less conspicuous event than it is.[28]

[28] Hannay, *Life of Smollett*, pp. 38–39. In his *Short History of the Royal Navy*
(London, 1898–[1909], II, 80–97, "The Men and the Life") Hannay gives an excellent summary of the conditions in the English navy when Smollett served. Compared

Rowlandson

Battle between Rod: Random and the Midshipman

In one respect, however, Smollett as a novelist of sea life was unique. Whereas Swift, Defoe, and others imitated the chronologies, logs, letters, authorities, personal allusions, and circumstantial details that established the genuineness of a travel book, Smollett turned his travels into fiction with so much sharpness of satiric intent that he was moved to omit all the factual earmarks of a travel book. He wished that his satire not be mistaken for libel, and, with the distinction between the two clearly in mind, he wrote: "Every intelligent reader will, at first sight, perceive I have not deviated from nature in the facts, which are all true in the main, although the circumstances are altered and disguised, to avoid personal satire."[29] As used in this passage, the facts are obviously the characters, incidents, and details of the story; hence Smollett wished to distinguish between the facts of a narrative which are true to nature, that is, universally true, and facts that are scientifically or historically true. The first category has to be presented imaginatively; the second must be supported statistically or historically. Smollett obviously realized that the novelist may learn from the voyager, or historian, or scientist but that ultimately he must universalize his interpretation and, in Wordsworth's words, carry "sensation into the midst of the objects of science itself."

This analysis of Smollett's conscious practice is tantamount to saying what is obvious when understood: that Smollett sorted his experiences by the moral and artistic standards of an educated Scottish landsman suddenly thrust into the ingrained brutality and incompetence of a British navy nearly at its lowest ebb and that he brought learning, experience, imagination, and literary powers to bear on the narrative of his own travel experiences without deviating "from nature in the facts"—without departing from artistic verisimilitude in incident, plot, or character.

---

with what Hannay presents, even the darkest passages in Smollett are, if anything, rather mild. For a comment on Smollett's account, see Thomas Carlyle, *Frederick the Great*, XII, xii.

[29] *Roderick Random*, I, xlii.

CHAPTER III

A RETIRED ADMIRAL

THE popular reception of *Roderick Random* encouraged Smollett, who early in 1750 was hard pressed financially, to undertake a second novel, the *Adventures of Peregrine Pickle*. Again he resorted to recollections of the navy and developed the first half of his novel by creating the characters of Commodore Hawser Trunnion, Lieutenant Jack Hatchway, and Boatswain Tom Pipes from the lives of three seamen, Admiral Daniel Hore, Captain John Bover, and Thomas Smale, whose naval careers and manner of retirement must have diverted and stimulated him.

Admiral Hore was identified as the original of Trunnion by the Reverend Edward Hinchliffe in his book *Barthomley: In Letters from a Former Rector to His Eldest Son*, published in 1856, over a hundred years after *Peregrine Pickle*. Hinchliffe was in many respects like Gilbert White, a churchman, a genealogist, and a local historian. The son and grandson of churchmen, he served in a parish where his father served before him and devoted his leisure to antiquarian studies, the results of which he cast in the form of letters. In the course of his remarks he describes a country home called "Bellefield" which Admiral Hore built in the neighborhood of Warrington, in Cheshire, and which in Hinchliffe's day was still standing. According to Hinchliffe, the Admiral chose

a site which commands a fine view of a richly wooded vale, backed by Halton Castle and Elsby Hills; and of the river Mersey—winding and widening its course to the sea; he there set to work to build a house; not after the fashion of an architect, but after the *model of a ship*. In it he had his cabins, and places, called by names which I, who am not a sailor, cannot venture to pronounce: and, before it, was a grass-plot, surrounded by a ha-ha, whereon he trudged for exercise, honouring it with the name of "quarter-deck." All who approached him there, were required to do so with their hats off, and with every other mark of respect and duty which belong to the reality. *Bells* sounded the time of day: and, as an *Admiral* on board his flag-ship, he breakfasted, dined, and supped, and went to bed. His movements were regulated by the weather-vane: in a kind of log-book, the points of the wind, and the occurrences of the day, were regularly noted down. His conversation about terrestrial things was always interlarded with nautical phraseology: on land he was at sea.[1]

Smollett doubtless first learned of Admiral Hore in the West Indies. In the Carthagena expedition Hore served as captain from July 28, 1740, until April 16, 1741, aboard the fireship "Success,"[2] which anchored at Carthagena April 4, 1741, when the fleet was in the midst of its operations in Carthagena harbor after the fall of Boca Chica. At five o'clock on the morning of April 17, Hore, in command of the captured Spanish ship "Gallicia," performed one of the most heroic and, through no fault of his own, futile maneuvers before Carthagena when, unaided by other ships, he was ordered to attack the sea walls of the town and for seven hours was bombarded by the Spanish until the "Gallicia" was so riddled that she almost sank under him. Smollett certainly heard of this operation and the gallant commander, for it was part of the crew of the "Chichester" who took over the "Gallicia" from the "Superbe," which had towed her in; four "Chichester" carpenters repaired her; "Chichester" casks of water, powder, and shot stocked her; and on April 12 a "Chichester" crew of a midshipman and fourteen men took charge of her. Surely some of the "Chichester" crew were among the three hundred volunteers that manned her in the attack.[3]

On April 17, 1741, the day on which he commanded the "Gallicia," Hore was transferred to the "Ludlow Castle"[4] and continued in command of her until October 11, 1741, when she was in Cumberland harbor. His next ship was the

---

[1] *Barthomley* (London, 1856), pp. 73-74.

[2] P.R.O., Ad. 36/3984. His first ship was the "Burford," the records of which are crumbling and incomplete.

[3] Watkins, "Journal," April 8-17, 1741.

[4] P.R.O., Ad. 36/1862.

"Defiance," of which there are no musters until 1745. He
entered the "Canterbury" on January 29, 1744,[5] his commission being dated February 8, and he quitted her January
29, 1747.[6] According to his log, during these years he sailed
from Plymouth to Louisburg, back to Spithead, and returned
to Louisburg to assist in the final attack in 1745; while at sea
he was constantly on the lookout for French ships which he
often chased. After the fall of Louisburg, he retired in 1748
to England for his health and within the following two years
built his strange house and settled in Appleton. In 1756 he
was entered on the superannuated list as a half-pay rear admiral, and six years later he died. Having described Bellefield,
the Admiral's home, Hinchliffe goes on to say of Hore that
"he was a rough, daring—every inch, a—sailor; and, at sea
or on land, in conversation or occupation, or in the arrangement of his house, never lost sight of the deepest nauticism
. . . . but, with all his professional foibles, not a warmer-
hearted, kinder, or more hospitable creature ever existed."[7]
While accepting the identification and the sketch of Admiral
Hore at home on his Cheshire estate, one has the feeling,
nevertheless, that Hinchliffe added to Hore's portrait traits
found in Hawser Trunnion and that Hore in real life was not
precisely the same person he appears in *Peregrine Pickle*.

Hinchliffe's remarks on Admiral Hore were made in con-
nection with a biography of Hinchliffe's maternal grandfather, Captain John Bover, of whom he wrote:

> Capt. Bover was afterwards attached to the flagship of Admiral Hoare,
> when a friendship of more than ordinary intimacy sprang up between the
> Admiral and himself. . . . . [Bellefield] was built by the gallant sailor, in
> order to be near his friend, Captain Bover, who had settled at an adjoining
> place, called Stockton Lodge, having been appointed the naval superin-
> tendent of the Cheshire district.[8]

It seems never to have occurred to Hinchliffe, perhaps because he was speaking of an ancestor, that Captain Bover is
obviously the original of Smollett's Lieutenant Hatchway.
The son of a Huguenot refugee, De Beauvoir by name, Bover

5 P.R.O., Ad. 36/463 and 465.   7 *Barthomley*, pp. 73–74.

6 P.R.O., Ad. 51/161.   8 *Ibid.*, pp. 73–74.

early entered the navy and steadily advanced until he was a post captain. Later he became successively naval superintendent of the Cheshire district, commander of the "Buckingham" in Byng's ill-starred expedition, and eventually regulating captain of Newcastle-upon-Tyne. Hinchliffe speaks often of Bover's polished manners and of the high respect shown him at his death in 1782. Bover married well and had thirteen children, three of his five sons distinguishing themselves in their father's profession.

To Hinchliffe's account of Captain Bover the following can now be added. John Bover entered the "Canterbury" during Hore's command, on February 20, 1745, and was commissioned a second lieutenant on September 30.[9] The last entry in Hore's log, September 17, 1747, while the "Canterbury" was at anchor in Louisburg harbor, records the transfer of John Bover to the "Norwich."[10] He had already been entered in the "Norwich" musters on August 29; on July 23, 1748, he was made a first lieutenant, a post which he held until March, 1749, when he left the "Norwich."[11] In the incomplete records of the "Raven," his name does not appear.[12] Of the Admiral's affection for Captain Bover there is record in the former's will, dated March 4, 1758, with a codicil of May 4, 1762, "proved in the Consistory Court of Chester on the 23rd day of August 1762." After remembering his family, Hore goes on to say: "I Give to Capt John Bover late of His Majesty's Sloop The Raven Thirty pounds a year during his natural life . . . . my gold head cane & Admiral Warrens gold mourning ring." He also appointed the Captain one of his three executors. It is pleasant to find that a friendship begun aboard the "Canterbury" in 1745 and celebrated by Smollett in 1750 was still warm and intimate twelve years later in Cheshire.

[9] P.R.O., Ad. 36/465, No. 210.

[10] P.R.O., Ad. 51/161.

[11] P.R.O., Ad. 36/2285, No. 602.

[12] P.R.O., Ad. 36/2822, unfit for use; Ad. 36/2823, covers the years 1745–48, and Ad. 36/6431, from 1753 to 1755. The only other record of any command by Bover is of the "Buckingham" from 1755 to 1756 (P.R.O., Ad. 36/5003). Hinchliffe believed the friendship between the two men began on the "Buckingham," but on this point he was apparently misinformed.

Finally, the Admiral's will helps to identify the original of Tom Pipes, the third in the trio of the Garrison in *Peregrine Pickle*. Of the several retainers remembered by Hore in his will, at least one was a servant of longstanding. Early in the will he makes the following bequest: "I give to my servant Thomas Smale fifteen pounds a year dureing his natural life & to him all my hounds & to be kept for him one year if he can't before that time sell them well," and later, when disposing of his household goods and stock, which were to be sold and the proceeds divided into three shares, he requested the largest share to go to Thomas Smale "and Jane Holland my house-keeper"; not satisfied with this bounty, he added that the share of these two be larger by forty pounds than the second share. Undoubtedly, this was the same Thomas Smale, boatswain's servant to John Gier, who was discharged from the "Lark" into the "Canterbury" on March 17, 1744, and who served there under Hore's command until April 27, 1745.[13]

What further parallels Smollett may have drawn from the lives of Daniel Hore, John Bover, and Thomas Smale, their long association, and their activities in Cheshire is not known. Did he, for example, when he concocted the wedding scene in *Peregrine Pickle*, have in mind the Admiral's horse Neptune, which was willed to Miss Ann Warburton of Arley, and the pack of hounds that passed to Thomas Smale? Moreover, there is no information as to how intimately Smollett knew these three men, if at all, or how he learned of their friendship and association. There is one possibility. Perhaps he may have passed near their residence in Cheshire if he traveled the Great Western Road when he journeyed to Aberdeen to receive from Marischal College a medical degree in June, 1750. If he rested for the night near Warrington, he may have heard an innkeeper tell, exactly as the innkeeper in *Peregrine Pickle* told Gamaliel Pickle, of a new dwelling in the immediate vicinity called "Bellefield," only recently built, or per-

---

[13] P.R.O., Ad. 36/465, No. 279. Smale served aboard the "Lark" from March 19, 1741, to March 17, 1744, but whether or not Hore commanded the "Lark" during this period has not been ascertained.

Commodore Trunnion & Lt. Hatchway engaged in a Fox-chace

haps even then under construction. But this is only a conjecture. After the alterations made by many generations,
Bellefield retains today but little of the original marine architecture, and the moat is almost filled. The literary pilgrim is
put to it to visualize Commodore Hawser Trunnion, Lieutenant Jack Hatchway, and Boatswain Tom Pipes in the farm-
yard, orchard, and cottage of an undistinguished English
farm, or to find in the lives of Admiral Hore, Captain Bover,
and Boatswain's Servant Thomas Smale all the versatility,
color, and humor of the Garrison. For again Smollett, with
all the richness of his experience and imagination, created
from a few sailors and an amusing situation great and original characters—ancients who pass their declining years, as
old sailors are wont to do, in recollections of their youthful
exploits. Admiral Hore's log of the "Canterbury" furnishes
glimpses of the strenuous and dangerous life the three led together while sailing the seas to many ports and ever in pursuit of the French, and *Peregrine Pickle* tells an unforgettable
story of a congenial reunion ashore in an amphibian dwelling,
where Hawser Trunnion, Jack Hatchway, and Tom Pipes are
free to relive the stirring days afloat.

Once more, as in *Roderick Random*, Smollett fell under the
spell of Shakespeare's soldiers in the *Henry V* trilogy and
particularly of Falstaff as interpreted on the contemporary
stage by James Quin. Of all the characters of his novels, Commodore Trunnion is endowed with the largest share of the
Falstaffian side of life. Both Trunnion and Falstaff have
grown old in service, both are strong characters dominating
the group in which they move, both are given to bragging of
past deeds and present courage, and both are called "old
lads of the castle": Falstaff from his original, Sir John Old-
castle, and Trunnion from his unique dwelling. Falstaff depends in his projects on Poins, whose sharp tongue he dreads;
he endures Poins's satiric thrusts at his tall tales and boast-
ings and he falls a victim to Poins's tricks—but with it all he
can still exclaim, "If the rascal have not given me medicines
to make me love him, I'll be hanged."[14] Trunnion stands in

[14] *1 Henry IV*, II, ii, 18-20.

almost exactly the same relation to Hatchway, depending on his company, fidelity, and aid, and also suffering from the mate's sharp tongue and love of a practical joke. The Commodore holds much affection for his servant, but it falls to Hatchway to use Falstaff's words, when he says, at Peregrine's departure, " 'I'll be d——n'd if the dog ha'n't given me some stuff to make me love him.' "[15]

There are other agreements. Captain Pistol is missing, having appeared earlier in *Roderick Random* as Captain Weazel; but Nym lives with all his taciturnity in Tom Pipes. One cannot but feel also that, consciously or unconsciously, Smollett modeled the deathbed scene of Commodore Trunnion on Falstaff's death. Both men in their last words speak from the heart; there is the same mingling of pathos and humor, the same momentary sobering effect on the servants. Bardolph's benediction, " 'Would I were with him, wheresome'er he is, either in heaven or in hell!' "[16] is echoed in Pipes's few words, " 'A better commander I'd never desire to serve; and who knows but I may help to set up thy standing rigging in another world?' "[17]

The transformation of Admiral Daniel Hore, Captain John Bover, and Boatswain's Servant Thomas Smale into Commodore Trunnion, Lieutenant Hatchway, and Boatswain Pipes exemplifies Smollett's handling of the naval material in *Peregrine Pickle*. He moved further away from personal experiences and satiric indignation into the realm of the imagination and the robust spirit of the comedy of humors. He drew upon his knowledge of the navy, no longer in the manner of voyagers, but in the spirit of Shakespeare and Jonson and Rabelais and Cervantes, with whom, in this respect at least, he may be compared to advantage. His greatest skill was in appropriating the idiom of sailors, heightening and enriching it until it became expressive and vigorous lan-

---

[15] *Peregrine Pickle*, I, 106.

[16] *Henry V*, II, iii, 6–7.

[17] *Peregrine Pickle*, III, 20. The foregoing details on the Shakespearean borrowing are taken from a fuller discussion in the *Parrot Presentation Volume* (Princeton, 1935), pp. 412–13.

guage. Magnified in word and deed, endowed with great vitality, Trunnion, Hatchway, and Pipes are no longer everyday sailors one meets on boats and wharves; they are nautical men writ large. Strange and grotesque though the facts may be, *Peregrine Pickle* departs no less from nature than does *Roderick Random*.

Far-reaching as are these artistic metamorphoses, ultimately they are dependent in their perfection on intimate knowledge, personal experience, and sympathy. If Smollett wrote the first English novel of the sea, it was because he was the first novelist to sail before the mast, and all his successors —Conrad, Marryat, Stevenson, Masefield—were also schooled on salt water.

CHAPTER IV

A CLASSICIST ON THE GRAND TOUR

TRUE to "the disposition of the Scots," Smollett was "addicted to travelling," but after his adventures in the British navy and perhaps a second visit to the West Indies, he was content to read the books of the voyagers and did not, according to extant records, venture again on the high seas. Instead he crossed the English Channel and made the Grand Tour, not once but several times. Among his contemporaries there was no institution of social culture so firmly established, no form of foreign travel so popular, as the Grand Tour. Sooner or later almost everyone with any pretentions or reputation in literature went abroad, and, numerous as were the journals and logs of voyagers, they were outnumbered by the books written by the British who traveled abroad. More will be said in chapter vii on the books that grew out of the Grand Tour and Smollett's excellent *Travels through France and Italy*. For the time being it is to be remembered that, when Smollett utilized the Grand Tour for prose fiction, he was not simply reverting to personal experience; he was taking up a subject of immediate, even widespread, contemporary interest.

As noted in a preceding chapter, Smollett, on his own authority, traveled "in France and other foreign countries," sometime before May, 1744.[1] John Shebbeare, his tireless critic, who can be trusted for a fact but not for an opinion, may have been alluding to the same tour when he said that

---

[1] *Letters*, pp. 6 and 80.

Smollett spent six weeks abroad, though it is possible that the visit Shebbeare had in mind came later, in 1748, when Smollett was preparing to translate Cervantes.[2] Other than these two allusions, there are no records of this early visit to the Continent, but the results are manifest in *Roderick Random*.

It will be recalled that, following the wreck of the "Lizard" and a short sojourn in Sussex, the hero of *Roderick Random* flees to France and after traveling about enlists in the army. He eventually participates in the military campaign which culminated in the Battle of Dettingen on June 16, 1743. Although Smollett thus drew upon a second historical incident very much as he had earlier utilized the Carthagena campaign, the fact does not imply that he himself witnessed the battle from the ranks of either the British or the French army. Yet his version of the battle agrees with accounts of other eyewitnesses,[3] and his interest in the event was more than casual, for later in the same book he introduced it in a coffee-house argument and drew a minor incident from it for an illustration in *Humphry Clinker*.[4]

One episode of Roderick's travels in France, however, Smollett clearly developed from a friendly encounter with a Scottish priest. Shortly after his arrival in Boulogne, Roderick finds his uncle, Captain Bowling, and through him meets a priest of Scottish extraction who labors doggedly to convert Roderick to Catholicism. The priest in turn introduces Roderick to Frère Balthazar, who becomes Roderick's traveling companion but who eventually decamps, having scandalized Roderick with his licentiousness. Not content with this one allusion to the priest, Smollett again mentions him in *Peregrine Pickle*, this time revealing his name. Peregrine, even in the few hours of passage through Boulogne, is dispatched by Smollett to visit

old Father Graham, a Scottish gentleman of the governor's acquaintance, who had lived as a capuchin in that place for the space of three score years,

[2] See n. 2, p. 12.

[3] *Report on the Manuscripts of the Duke of Buccleuch*, I, 402-4.

[4] *Humphry Clinker*, I, 135.

and during that period conformed to all the austerities of the order with the most rigorous exactness; being equally remarkable for the frankness of his conversation, the humanity of his disposition, and the simplicity of his manners.[5]

Finally, when in 1763 he was in Boulogne again, nearly twenty years after the first visit, Smollett recalled in a reminiscent mood Father Graham and memorialized him in the *Travels*. On this occasion he intimates that, in spite of good Father Graham, his Capuchin monastery never seemed to have escaped the temptations of the flesh. The passage in the *Travels*, though long, is quoted to illustrate how lasting and intimate was the personal experience that lay back of Roderick's Boulogne adventure:

In the Lower Town of Boulogne there are several religious houses, particularly a seminary, a convent of Cordeliers, and another of Capuchins. This last, having fallen to decay, was some years ago repaired, chiefly by the charity of British travellers, collected by father Graeme, a native of North-Britain, who had been an officer in the army of king James II. and is said to have turned monk of this mendicant order, by way of voluntary penance, for having killed his friend in a duel. Be that as it may, he was a well-bred, sensible man, of a very exemplary life and conversation; and his memory is much revered in this place. . . . . I often walk in the garden of the convent, the walls of which are washed by the sea at high-water. At the bottom of the garden is a little private grove, separated from it by a high wall, with a door of communication; and hither the Capuchins retire, when they are disposed for contemplation. About two years ago, this place was said to be converted to a very different use. There was among the monks one *père Charles*, a lusty friar, of whom the people tell strange stories. Some young women of the town were seen mounting over the wall, by a ladder of ropes, in the dusk of the evening; and there was an unusual crop of bastards that season. In short, *père Charles* and his companions gave such scandal, that the whole fraternity was changed; and now the nest is occupied by another flight of these birds of passage.[6]

Were the "two years" of the *Travels* twenty years, Père Charles might be considered the original of Frère Balthazar; but, as it is, Smollett's memories of a chance acquaintance in Boulogne before 1748 gave Father Graham and one of his Capuchins a memorable chapter in *Roderick Random*, a passing allusion in *Peregrine Pickle*, and a paragraph in the *Travels*.

Elsewhere in *Roderick Random* Smollett has little to say of

<hr>

[5] *Peregrine Pickle*, II, 11–12.   [6] *Travels*, pp. 19–20.

the sights on the road that Roderick traveled from Boulogne through Abbeville and Amiens to the Coq d'Or at Noyon; he rather concentrates on Roderick's contacts with French religious orders and his service in the French army before and after the Battle of Dettingen. If Smollett had any discernible purpose in these chapters, it was to delineate the character of the French soldier rather than to appeal to a topical interest in the battle, and his observations are little more than the usual outbursts of British prejudice on liberty, patriotism, valor, or honor common to his contemporaries.

It was in his second novel, *Peregrine Pickle*, written after a second and more extended tour in France in 1750, that Smollett made the richest use of the Grand Tour as a subject for prose fiction. The first quarter of the novel, it will be recalled, is dominated mostly by Hawser Trunnion and his crew, but while the seamen are advancing in years and their humor is wearing thin, young Peregrine is growing up as a student in Winchester and Oxford and eventually takes the Grand Tour to complete his education. After his departure the Commodore and his crew retire into the background, and the young adventurer sets out on his "peregrinations," which, true to his name, are destined to involve him in many "pickles." Attended by a French valet, his tutor Jolter, and secretly by Pipes, Peregrine takes leave of Trunnion, whose salty words of advice are every bit as good as his deathbed farewell, and, crossing the channel amid the usual storm, travels up to Paris through Calais, Boulogne, Bernay, Abbeville, Amiens, Chantilly, to a hotel in the *faubourg* St.-Germain, from which he later moves to private quarters in the Académie de Palfrenier, where he remains for fifteen months. At the end of this period he returns to England along the much-traveled route through Arras, Lille, Menin, Courtrai, Ghent, Melle, Alost, Brussels, Antwerp, Rotterdam, Maas, The Hague, Amsterdam, Leiden, Hellevoetsluis, and Haarlem, arriving finally in England at Harwich. There is hardly a subject connected with the Grand Tour upon which Peregrine does not touch, from Shakespeare's Cliff at Dover to the rough crossing, deceitful seamen, ragamuffin porters, haughty custom inspectors, rapacious publicans, begging friars, Englishmen in Paris, all classes of Frenchmen and Dutchmen from lord to peasant, and all the sights of city and country. Indeed, the second quarter of *Peregrine Pickle* is one great, sustained prose satire on the Grand Tour, every detail of which can be fully substantiated from contemporary books on Continental travel, of which more will be said in relation to Smollett's *Travels;* but one need go no further than Professor Mead's able survey, *The Grand Tour in the Eighteenth Century,* for a comprehensive commentary on Peregrine's travels.[7]

When Smollett reached the point in the novel where Peregrine sets out for the Continent, Smollett himself packed his bags and, according to Robert Anderson, went abroad "to survey the characters of mankind on a new theatre, and in greater variety than he had hitherto had any opportunity of viewing them in the capital of England."[8] Some of the details of the tour are preserved by another biographer, Dr. John Moore, who knew Smollett and was in Paris during Smollett's visit. There are also a number of allusions in the *Travels* to the 1750 tour. Among the topics mentioned either by Moore or in the *Travels* which are repeated by Smollett in *Peregrine Pickle* are the encounter with the exiles of the Rebellion of 1745[9] and Father Graham (or Graeme),[10] the quarrel over Mme Maintenon and the English victories,[11] the adventure with the French *traiteur* and his wife,[12] the murder of the nervous barber,[13] and the character of Pallet. Such parallels between Smollett's experiences and *Peregrine Pickle* are

[7] William Edward Mead, *The Grand Tour in the Eighteenth Century* (Boston, 1914). The following chapters apply to *Peregrine Pickle:* "The English Channel," pp. 29–31; "French Roads," pp. 44–45; "French Inns," pp. 78–84; "The Tourist and the Tutor," pp. 103–39, and "The Low Countries," pp. 364–74.

[8] *Life of Smollett,* p. 39.

[9] *Peregrine Pickle,* II, 13–16; cf. Moore, *Life,* pp. 94–95.

[10] *Peregrine Pickle,* II, 11–12; cf. *Travels,* pp. 19–20.

[11] *Peregrine Pickle,* II, 140–41; cf. *Travels,* p. 38.

[12] *Peregrine Pickle,* II, 26–27; cf. *Travels,* pp. 58–59.

[13] *Peregrine Pickle,* II, 35–36; cf. Moore, *Life,* p. 95. See also *Travels,* pp. 25, 48, and 49 for further references to the tour of 1750.

limited by our general ignorance of Smollett's life; incidents might be multiplied were more known of his travels.

Again, as in *Roderick Random*, the contrast in characters heightens the appeal of the incidents. Jolter, the vulgar, pedantic tutor, in his low tastes, his ignorance, and his treatment of his charge embodies one of the most common and most often satirized characters taking the Grand Tour. He also appears as a representative of that group of Englishmen who championed all things French; hence out of his efforts to instruct his English pupil arise the many contrasts between English and French life which Smollett introduces to the constant prejudice of the French. As soon as Peregrine and Jolter land, quarrels begin over French politeness and range over peasants, polite society, the nobility, justice, soldiers, boxing, gallantry, government, and manners.

In the Palais-Royal, Peregrine comes across two fellow-countrymen whose surprising manners promise "something entertaining." One is an old gentleman, Pallet by name, a London painter who has stolen a fortnight from his work to visit the galleries of France and Flanders. He "strutted in a gay summer dress of the parisian cut," carried his hat with a red feather under his arm, and loquaciously passed judgment with much assurance and ignorance on the works of the masters. Pallet exemplifies a class of travelers frequent in Smollett's day but even more numerous later—persons who are ambitious to turn connoisseur but whose qualifications embrace little more than a smattering of information distorted by presumptuous and misguided enthusiasm. It adds little to the authenticity of the character to learn that Smollett drew Pallet from a flesh-and-blood model. Smollett's biographer, Moore, writes:

> The painter whom Smollett afterwards typified under the name of Pallet, was in the capital of France at that time [1750]. This man used to declaim, with rapture, on the subject of *virtu*, and, as Smollett declared, often used the following expression: *"Paris is very rich in the arts. London is a Goth, and Westminster a Vandal, compared to Paris."* This preference, with the pert manners of the man, disgusted Smollett, and he exhibited Pallet in the "Adventures of Peregrine Pickle."[14]

[14] *Life*, pp. 93–94.

Smollett has expanded the painter's favorite observation into the following speech of Pallet's:

"France, to be sure, is rich in the arts; but what is the reason? The King encourages men of genius with honour and rewards; whereas, in England, we are obliged to stand upon our own feet, and combat the envy and malice of our brethren—egad! I have a good mind to come and settle here in Paris; I should like to have an apartment in the Louvre, with a snug pension of so many thousand livres."[15]

Although the character Pallet is modeled on an actual person, it is entirely fallacious to conclude that Smollett's purpose extended no further than personal satire. Connoisseurship, virtuosity, and false enthusiasm were discussed in polite society throughout the century. No subject was closer to the heart of the Grand Tour than criticism of art, and it occupies a prominent place in most travel books. Later, in his *Travels*, Smollett iterated that he had no pretensions to be a connoisseur,[16] and his strictures on enthusiasm[17] and the virtuosos[18] were outspoken. For these reasons, it is wisest to say that Smollett satirized in Pallet not an individual but enthusiastic and ignorant English criticism of art.[19] Yet even here an exception must be made. Pallet is a well-rounded figure; he has much to say on a variety of subjects; and, when these comments do not involve art, he renders good, common-sense decisions. At times he even arouses sympathy in the reader, and on at least one occasion in "The Entertainment in the Manner of the Ancients" his reactions represent the consensus of British taste in Smollett's day.

A second contemporary of Smollett, Dr. Mark Akenside, was portrayed in *Peregrine Pickle* in the character of the Doctor.[20] He appears as "a young man, in whose air and countenance appeared all the uncouth gravity and super-

---

[15] *Peregrine Pickle*, II, 56–57.

[16] *Travels*, pp. 87, 90, 223, 234, 235, 240, 250, 251, 252, 281, and 287.

[17] *Ibid.*, p. 41.   [18] *Ibid.*, pp. 234 and 240.

[19] Cf. Goldsmith's *Citizen of the World*, Letter XXXIV, "Of the Present Ridiculous Passion of the Nobility for Painting" (*Works*, ed. J. W. M. Gibbs [London, 1884–86], III, 129–33), for the same sort of satire.

[20] The identification was first made by Moore (*Life*, p. 94) and accepted by all later biographers.

cilious self-conceit of a physician piping hot from his studies."[21] It has been assumed that Smollett caricatured Akenside because of Akenside's uncomplimentary remarks on
Scotland,[22] yet the Doctor in *Peregrine Pickle* is never involved
in any situation directly related to Scotland,[23] and if Smollett
were satirizing Akenside on this score, surely he would have
had him disgraced by a Scotsman and not by Pallet and Jolter only. Unquestionably, Smollett wrote in the vein of the
chronique scandaleuse and enlivened the second half of *Peregrine Pickle* with personal satire, but it does not follow that
Smollett had in mind either intention in his description of
Akenside. The caricature touches only Akenside's public
life, and it neither impugns his scholarship nor exaggerates
any of his traits—in fact, the correspondences between Akenside and the Doctor are, as Professor Buck has shown,
"broadly perfect."[24] To accept either the personal or the
journalistic motive for Smollett's treatment of Akenside is to
overlook the fact that, in the portrayal of the Doctor, Smollett represents him as an out-and-out classicist; he is a traveling Tory of the old school who compares all he sees with his
beloved classics and invariably finds the moderns wanting.

In the talk of the Doctor ("a mere index-hunter," in Peregrine's estimation, "who held the eel of science by the tail"),[25]
Jolter the tutor, Pallet the staunch Englishman, and Peregrine, every new subject is canvassed from the three points
of view—classic, French, and English. The controversy begins in the Palais-Royal on the question of ancient versus
modern painting, later continues on questions of government,
warfare, the stage, taste, and dueling, and reaches its real

[21] *Peregrine Pickle*, II, 53.

[22] Moore, *Life*, p. 94; Chambers, *Smollett*, pp. 55–56; and Buck, "Smollett and
Dr. Akenside," *Journal of English and Germanic Philosophy*, XXXI (January, 1932),
22–23.

[23] The Doctor does quarrel with a Scottish officer but only on the topic of ancient
versus modern military tactics. When the Doctor feels himself vanquished, he includes in "an answer full of virulence . . . . a national reflection upon the soldier's
country" (*Peregrine Pickle*, II, 114). No more mention is made of Scotland.

[24] "Smollett and Dr. Akenside," *Journal of English and Germanic Philology*,
XXXI, 13, 18–19.

[25] *Peregrine Pickle*, II, 56.

culmination in "The Entertainment in the Manner of the Ancients."

Smollett set the stage very carefully for his great contest of the ancient versus the modern culinary arts. Peregrine becomes only a spectator, but the moderns are well represented in a French marquis, an Italian count, a German baron, and Pallet, each reacting according to the accepted habits of his nation, while arrayed against them is the classicist host and cook, the Doctor. Meanwhile faint rumblings of the storm that is brewing come from the kitchen, where the French cooks are in rebellion over mixing oil with honey, and only one can be bribed and awed into taking orders. Difficulty is also experienced in seating the guests on the Roman lounges, but the crowning moment arrives for the Doctor when he introduces each of his dishes with a learned résumé of the recipe. Here are some of the courses: " 'boiled goose, served up in a sauce composed of pepper, lovage, coriander, mint, rue, anchovies, and oil!' " the salacacabia, " 'a curious hashis of the lights, liver, and blood of a hare,' " dormice pie, " 'a sow's stomach, filled with a composition of minced pork, hog's brains, eggs, pepper, cloves, garlic, anniseed, rue, ginger, oil, wine, and pickle,' " " 'a fricassee of snails, fed, or rather purged, with milk,' " all ending in a dessert of "candied assafoetida."[26] No wonder the smell, as well as the savor, of the viands threw the good Doctor's guests into spasms and caused unfortunate accidents. Pallet, whose reactions and objections are the most violent, becomes the champion of the moderns, and the Doctor wages a losing battle. All agree with Pallet when he exclaims that "he would not give one slice of the roast beef of Old England for all the dainties of a Roman emperor's table."[27]

Once the humor is forgotten and the revulsion at these strange dishes has worn off, the reader is left to marvel at Smollett's imagination or his learning. His wonder is somewhat qualified by respect when he learns that "The Entertainment in the Manner of the Ancients" originated in a famous Latin cookbook ascribed to Marcus Gabius Apicius

[26] *Ibid.*, pp. 70–76.　　　　　　[27] *Ibid.*, p. 73.

Feast after the manner of the Antients

Rowlandson

and completed in the latter part of the third century A.D. Apicius was a famous—almost apocryphal—gourmet, who lived approximately from 14 B.C. to A.D. 37 and who spent a large fortune on food. Because of his reputation, his name was affixed to a collection of recipes, some of Greek origin and others concocted as late as the third century.[28] The collection was often copied and later edited, notably by Gabriel Humelbergius (Zurich, 1542), by Martin Lister (London, 1705), and by Theodore Jansson van Almeloveen (Amsterdam, 1709). Lister's edition, which was based on Humelbergius' and in turn was reprinted with few additions by Almeloveen, is a rare and learned book with the commanding title: *Apicii Coelii de Opsoniis et Condimentis, Sive Arte Coquinaria, Libri Decem. Cum Annotationibus Martini Lister, ē Medicis domesticis serenissimae Majestatis Reginae Annae. Et Notis selectioribus variisque lectionibus integris, Humelbergii, Caspari Barthii & Variorum.*

This Latin cookbook, either in Lister's or in Almeloveen's edition,[29] supplied Smollett with all his information on Roman foods. His close adherence to his source in the account of the feast may be illustrated by three of the many parallels. The banquet opens appropriately with soup, served by the Doctor with these words:

"At each end [of the table] there are dishes of the salacacabia of the Romans; one is made of parsley, pennyroyal, cheese, pinetops, honey,

[28] Frederick Vollmer, *Studien zu dem römischen Kochbuche von Apicius* (Munich, 1920), and Joseph Dommers Vehling, *Apicius, Cookery and Dining in Ancient Rome* (Chicago, 1930), *passim*.

[29] From Smollett's quotations and paraphrases it is impossible to determine which edition lay before him, the London edition of Lister or the Amsterdam edition of Almeloveen. At the close of the banquet the Doctor served the dessert with the assertion that candied asafetida "in contradiction to Aumelbergius and Lister, was no other than the *laser Syriacum*" (*Peregrine Pickle*, II, 76), but the fact that Smollett did not mention Almeloveen does not necessarily mean that Smollett did not employ his edition. First of all, "Aumelbergius" may, in fact, be a corruption of "Humelbergius" made under the influence of Almeloveen, and, second, only Humelbergius and Lister debate the "laser Syriacum" question in both editions. The point is a minor one, and, while the allusion is not specific in one respect, it does make certain that Smollett used a copy of Lister's edition as published either in London or in Amsterdam, and until evidence is found to the contrary all references will be made to Lister's edition of Apicius' *De opsoniis et condimentis* (London, 1705).

vinegar, brine, eggs, cucumbers, onions, and hen livers; the other is much the same as the soup-maigre of this country."[30]

With this compare the first recipe of Book IV, "Qui Pandecter appellatur":

Salacacabia. Piper, mentham, apium, pulegium aridum, caseum, nucleos pineos: mel, acetum, liquamen, ovorum vitella, aquam recentem, conteres: panem ex posca maceratum exprimes; caseum bubulum: cucumeres in cacubulo compones, interpositis nucleis, mittes concisas cepas aridas minutim, jecuscula gallinarum, jus profundes, super frigidam collocabis, & sic appones.

Aliter salacacabia Apiciana. Adjicies in mortario apii semen, pulegium aridum, mentham aridam, zingiber, coriandrum viridem, uvam passam enucleatam: mel, acetum, oleum & vinum: conteres. Adjicies in cacabulo panis Picentini tria frusta: interpones pulpas pulli, glandulas hedinas, caseum Vestinum, nucleos pineos, cucumeres, cepas aridas minutè concisas: jus superfundes. Insuper nivem sub ora asperges, & inferes.[31]

The Doctor's description of his main dish is derived in part from the text, in part from the commentary:

"This here, gentleman, is a boiled goose, served up in a sauce composed of pepper, lovage, coriander, mint, rue, anchovies, and oil! I wish, for your sakes, gentlemen, it was one of the geese of Ferrara, so much celebrated among the ancients for the magnitude of their livers, one of which is said to have weighed upwards of two pounds; with this food, exquisite as it was, did the tyrant Heliogabulus regale his hounds."[32]

Apicius in chapter viii, Book VI, is briefer:

Anserem elixum calidum è jure frigido Apiciano. Teres piper, ligusticum, coriandrum, mentham, tutam, refundis liquamen, & oleum modicè, temperas Anserem elixum ferventem, Sabano mundo exiccabis, jus perfundis, & inferes.

To this enumeration Lister adds sundry details, some of which were adopted by Smollett:

Anserem elixum ferventem.] Ex aqua coctum. Miror nostrum Apicium hic non meminisse jecoris anseris farsilis, cùm peculiariter hîc egerit de ansere elixo ex jure Apiciano. Fortè hujus silentii in causa fuit, quòd plurimi sibi vindicabant istiusmodi inventum; uti suprà citavit ex Plinio Humelbergius.

Hepar tamen Anserinum exquisitissimum cibi genus Romæ habetur. Athenæus. Archestratus autem altilis anseris pullum simul cum parente jubet apparari, eumque assari simpliciter. Idem.

Canes jecoribus anserum pavit Heliogabalus. Lampridius: an ex os-

[30] Peregrine Pickle, II, 70–71.

[31] De opsoniis et condimentis, p. 89.   [32] Peregrine Pickle, II, 70.

tentatione infinitæ luxuriæ, & ad derisionem inventionis; an quòd anserum carnes impuræ Syris fuerunt, ut Judæis & Britannis nostris? Antonius Musa Brassivolus refert (com. I. in Hipp. de ratione victûs in acutis) refert Ferrariæ Anseres fartiles suo tempore fuisse, quorum hepar duas libras quandoque pendebat. Ut autem illud in molem excrescerat, ficubus illos, non secus ac porcos alebant. Hujus rei rationem vide apud Stenonem sua Anatomiâ hepatis Anserini.[33]

One fish sauce in particular disgusted the Doctor's guests:

. . . . the celebrated *garum* of the Romans; that famous pickle having been prepared sometimes of the *scombri*, which were a sort of tunny-fish, and sometimes of the *silurus*, or shad-fish; nay, he observed that there was a third kind, called *garum hæmation*, made of the guts, gills, and blood of the *thynnus*.[34]

This short passage is based on a long commentary on Book I, chapter vii, "De liquamine emendando," part of which follows:

Liquamen si odorem malum fecerit: vas inane inversum fumiga lauro & cupresso, & in hoc liquamen funde ante ventilatum: Si salsum fuerit, mellis sextarium mittis, & move spica, & emendâsti. Sed & mustum recens idem præstat.

LISTER.

Liquamen.] Id est, Garum: *Quarum, quod appelamus* (nòs putà Africani, Cæl. Aurelianus Chronicon, lib. 2.) *liquamen è pisce Siluro confectum:* Nempe ex Sturione Niliaco; ubi omnium maximi capti fuerunt, teste Plinio, tanquam ejus fluminis peculiares essent: at nescio, an ullus alius scriptor istius confectionis mentionem fecerit; scilicet Gari è Siluro: *è scombris fit Garum excellentissimum;* . . . . [five hundred words].

"Præstantius porrò Garum *Hæmation* appelatum sic fit. Intestina Thynni cum branchiis cruoréque ac *sanguine* accipiuntur, aspergiturque salis quod satis est, & in vase sinuntur. Post menses duos fermè vas ipsum perforato, effluetque garum Hæmation appellatum." Hujus & superiorum meminit Martialis.

Antipolitani fateor, sum filia Thynni:
Essem, si Scombri non tibi missa forem.[35]

Smollett returned to the subject of garum again in his *Travels*. Here he wrote:

The famous pickle Garum was made from the *Thynnus* or *Tunny* as well as from the *Scomber*, but that from the *Scomber* was counted the most delicate. Commentators, however, are not agreed about the *Scomber* or *Scombrus*. Some suppose it was the *Herring* or *Sprat* [*sarda*]; others believe it was the mackarel [*scomber, scombri*]; after all, perhaps it was the *Anchovy*,

[33] *De opsoniis et condimentis*, pp. 145–46.

[34] *Peregrine Pickle*, II, 75.   [35] *De opsoniis et condimentis*, pp. 15–17.

which I do not find distinguished by any other Latin name: for the *Encrasicolus* is a Greek appellation altogether generical. Those who would be further informed about the *Garum* and the *Scomber* may consult *Cœlius Apicius de recogninaria, cum notis variorum.*[36]

Further parallels between *Peregrine Pickle* and Apicius would only corroborate what has already been demonstrated of Smollett's procedure in "The Entertainment in the Manner of the Ancients." No instance has been found where he supplemented Apicius with other material, though he made substitutions, such as *anchoys* for *liquamen*, a sauce often made of anchovies. Without once departing from his source book, he winnowed its material with the hand of a humorist for purposes of satire and comedy. He did not merely thumb through the index for preposterous foods and dishes but read the book thoroughly, and to trace his sources it has been necessary to read Apicius and his commentators closely. The relevant commentary on *garum*, for example, is added to the chapter on *liquamen* and is not indexed. Humelbergius' and Lister's erudite notes on *laser Cyrenaicum*, or *laser Syriacum* as Smollett calls it, are appended to chapter xxx, Book I, and the information that it sold "to the weight of a silver penny" is added in the commentary to chapter i, Book VII. Smollett ranged through the book and so mastered the subject that some years later when he was traveling abroad he was able to make informative observations on Roman food.[37]

To return now to the classicist and his banquet. As in all the scenes that involve the Doctor, the emphasis in the feast is not so much upon the Doctor's character as upon the comparative study of the ancients versus the moderns. The Doctor's "scandalous partiality" for the ancients, his learning, his ostentation, and his defeat are in keeping with all he says and does elsewhere. Perrault and Fontenelle had restricted

[36] *Travels*, p. 323. The passage is printed as corrected by Smollett in a copy, now in the British Museum, he prepared for a new edition. The Latin title is certainly a misprint for *de re coquinaria*, a shortened title frequently used for the book.

[37] *Travels*, pp. 157, 158, 160, 323-24. Cf. also the *Present State of All Nations*, II, 12, and the *Critical Review*, VIII (October, 1759), 284-89, a review doubtless by Smollett with allusions to Apicius. A very clever parody of the banquet is to be found in the early chapters of Vol. II of *The Life and Opinions of Bertram Montfichet, Esq.* (London, [1761]). Here the main dish is "Porcus Trojanus."

their comparisons between the ancients and the moderns to poetry, oratory, painting, and architecture; the Englishmen Temple, Swift, Boyle, Wotton, and Bentley had extended the quarrel to philosophy and science. Smollett, coming at a later date when interest in the Romans was shifting to the everyday life of the average Roman citizen, turned to more familiar matters and brought home the quarrel between the ancients and the moderns on a subject relished by all his contemporaries—the enjoyment of good food and drink.

After making the Grand Tour, Peregrine returned to London animated by an insolent pride and pretentious ambition. At this point in the novel Smollett speaks out and condemns his hero:

Sorry I am, that the task I have undertaken, lays me under the necessity of divulging this degeneracy in the sentiments of our imperious youth, who was now in the heyday of his blood, flushed with the consciousness of his own qualifications, vain of his fortune, and elated on the wings of imaginary expectation.[38]

The last two volumes of the novel, about half the entire work, trace Peregrine's discipline in the bitter school of experience until he reaches the lowest ebb of his fortunes in prison, whereupon Smollett again comments:

I might here, in imitation of some celebrated writers, furnish out a page or two, with the reflections he made upon the instability of human affairs, the treachery of the world, and the temerity of youth; and endeavour to decoy the reader into a smile, by some quaint observation of my own, touching the sagacious moraliser. But, besides that I look upon this practice as an impertinent anticipation of the peruser's thoughts, I have too much matter of importance upon my hands, to give the reader the least reason to believe that I am driven to such paltry shifts, in order to eke out the volume.[39]

Most readers may demur that Smollett has more than incurred his own censure by eking out two volumes with stupid adventure, disgraceful personal satire, and the inclusion of "The Memoirs of a Lady of Quality." Through all these later chapters the influence of travel was negligible. Peregrine's experiences in London and Bath are almost pure adventure with some topical allusions. The long digression on Mackercher's espousal of the suit of James Annesley for the

[38] *Peregrine Pickle*, II, 217.   [39] *Ibid.*, IV, 139.

title of Earl of Anglesey doubtless goes back to the Carthagena expedition, when Smollett may have met either or both
of these men and when Annesley as a common sailor first asserted his claim to the title.

Most readers and critics agree, I believe, that the first half
of *Peregrine Pickle* is more enjoyable than the second half
and that there is a falling-off in quality and originality after
the death of Trunnion and the return of Peregrine from the
Grand Tour. The theme changes from sea life and travel to
fashionable society, from character to incident, and for some
readers this shift may be for the better; but certainly Smollett's reputation and lasting appeal are founded not so much
on Peregrine and his escapades[40] as on Hawser Trunnion,
Jack Hatchway, Tom Pipes, Pallet, and the Doctor and on
the humors of seamen and of foreign travelers.

[40] There is one minor bit of evidence, however, that Peregrine was a recognized
type in English society, that his adventures were of everyday occurrence, and that
his manners and humor were acceptable. This testimony is to be found in the
Memoirs of William Hickey, ed. Alfred Spencer (London, 1913–25). Hickey's story
of his own youth parallels in kind but not in particulars almost every subject of the
last half of *Peregrine Pickle*. His commentary on the nickname given to him in 1754
applies with even more aptness to Peregrine. Hickey wrote: "By the time I was five
years of age, I got the nick name of 'PICKLE,' a name I fear I have through life
proved to have been but too well applied" (I, 6).

CHAPTER V

THE PROSE FICTION OF THE ARMCHAIR

IT WILL be recalled that in his second novel, *Peregrine Pickle*, Smollett profited by his voyage to the West Indies, his journey to Scotland, and a tour of France. Written in 1750, though published in 1751, this novel marks in a sense the culmination of a period in Smollett's life. Late in the summer of 1750 he took up his residence in Chelsea and for the ensuing twelve to thirteen years devoted his energies almost exclusively to journalism. During these years of sedentary toil he wrote but two novels, *Ferdinand Count Fathom* and *Sir Launcelot Greaves*, which succeeding generations have cared for less than his other prose fiction. Inasmuch as these novels were little influenced by the author's journalistic activities, they may therefore be considered first.

In *Ferdinand Count Fathom*, published in 1753, Smollett retained features of his first two novels and also essayed new methods and subjects. The results have generally been viewed with a critical disfavor which appears to spring, at least in part, from misunderstanding. Yet *Fathom* is memorable, among other things, for Smollett's statement of his conception of the novel:

A novel is a large diffused picture, comprehending the characters of life, disposed in different groups, and exhibited in various attitudes, for the purposes of an uniform plan, and general occurrence, to which every individual figure is subservient. But this plan cannot be executed with propriety, probability, or success, without a principal personage to attract the attention, unite the incidents, unwind the clue of the labyrinth, and at last close the scene, by virtue of his own importance.[1]

[1] *Ferdinand Count Fathom*, I, 3.

If any distinction between *Roderick Random*, *Peregrine Pickle*, and *Count Fathom* is to be observed in relation to this formula, it is to be noticed chiefly in the protagonists. In the first, Roderick, the Scottish adventuring traveler, represents "modest merit struggling with every difficulty to which a friendless orphan is exposed," and his hardships are designed to arouse in the reader sympathy rather than mirth. His intentions are generally commendable, but he is deficient in a sense of humor. In *Peregrine Pickle* the central figure stands at the opposite pole; favored by natural gifts and a wealthy uncle, he enjoys the fruit of the land and comes to grief through his pride and insolence. The reader is repelled, but not indignant, at his heartlessness and his overdeveloped love of horseplay.

Fathom, as Smollett further indicates in the Preface, belongs to a long line of thorough-paced villians, of which Shakespeare's Richard III and Congreve's Maskwell in the *Double Dealer* are consummate examples. Unlike these noble or fashionable characters, he is but a scheming, vicious sharper, whose ambition is to live in luxury without labor and to escape the vengeance of his victims, which compels him to be forever on the move. His character is not redeemed by either a sense of humor or of morality. "Chosen . . . . from the purlieus of treachery and fraud," he displays the proclivities of Richard and Maskwell, no longer in the "more limited field of invention" of the drama but expanded in "the large diffused picture" of the novel. Monimia, the leading female character, derives more than her name from Otway's *The Orphan;*[2] in both novel and play Monimia suffers the same misfortunes in her lovers, though Smollett has contrived a happy ending for his heroine's love and devotion. Renaldo, her true lover, even observes that his relation to Monimia and to Fathom bears a close resemblance to that of Polydore, Monimia, and Castalio in the play.[3] The influence of the stage extends to the theatrical settings for Fathom's melodramatic adventure during the storm in the forest near Paris

[2] *Ibid.*, II, 28.   [3] *Ibid.*, p. 58.

and Renaldo's reunion with Monimia in the English church.

Without further parallels, it is evident that in *Fathom* Smollett was turning from his own experiences to the drama for character, incident, and setting. Whether or not he was wise in imitating the drama is beyond the present purpose, but it is pertinent to remark that the atmosphere of the Restoration stage, with its concentration on the heroic or courtly to the exclusion of other walks of life, was foreign to Smollett's absorption in the realities of common everyday people. Furthermore, no matter what the play, the actor, through interpretation, actions, and voice, lends to the character on the stage the reality it may lack in line and deed. In the theater the illusion of reality must be maintained for only a few hours, and the audience, the stage machinery, music, lights, and pageantry divert the reason from analysis and release the fancy. In contrast, the novelist is dependent upon only the written word; he must create a "willing suspension of disbelief" over a long period with frequent interruptions, and he must create active and sustained characters. Smollett in his mind's eye doubtless pictured Monimia as Mrs. Cibber[4] and Fathom as Garrick playing Maskwell; but when he undertook to transfer these living actors to the pages of *Fathom*, he failed to create in words a reality to replace that of the tangible actor and stage.

In *Fathom* Smollett also indulges for the first time in a conscious elaboration of his style, quite clearly after the example of Fielding. He often steps aside from the narration to speak in his own person, to add reflections on the conduct of the characters or on life in general, and to expand titles of chapters until they become not only summaries but extensive commentaries as, "Their first Attempt; with a Digression which some Readers may think impertinent," "The Biter is bit," "The Mystery unfolded—Another Recognition, which, it is to be hoped, the Reader could not foresee." Finally, in a

---

[4] In *Peregrine Pickle* (II, 116) Smollett praised Mrs. Cibber as Monimia (cf. John Genest, *Some Account of the English Stage* [Bath, 1832], III, 496; IV, 184; V, 101) and he often celebrated Garrick in his villain roles.

digression entirely beside the point, Smollett, with his eye on
Fielding's Tom Jones, justifies his choice of a foundling for a
hero and his introduction of "low" scenes.[5]

Travel had only a secondary and desultory influence on
Fathom. In flight from his victims or in quest of new fields to
plunder, Fathom travels widely on the Continent and in England, and, though localities are often specified, there is, with
a few exceptions, a total absence of distinguishing features of
geography or society. The French forest scene and the English church are colorless as to time and place; Vienna, Paris,
London, Bath, Bristol Springs, and Tunbridge may, for the
general purpose and subject of the novel, be one and the same
place. The characters, too, though they hail from several
countries, are devoid of national traits; Renaldo is as much at
home in London as in Vienna, and Teresa and Elenor are of
the same cut, though one is a Hungarian and the other the
daughter of an English curate. In none of his novels did
Smollett have such varied opportunities for contrasting one
nationality with another, and in none did he have less to say
on the subject.[6]

The history of Fathom's birth, education, and early man-
hood up to the day when he enters the gates of Paris, though
carrying him through a diversity of scenes and many nationalities, is entirely lacking in local differentia; but, once
Fathom launches upon his career in Paris, he is attracted,
first of all, by the interplay of nationalities and forthwith
cultivates the attention of a Westphalian count, a Bolognian
marquis, a French abbé, a Dutch officer, and an English
squire.[7] Later, in a London prison, Fathom is thrown with
Scottish Sir Mungo Barebones, Irish Major Macleaver, English Captain Minikin, Theodore, king of Corsica, and the
crazed Frenchman.[8] In the scenes in both cities Smollett was

[5] *Fathom*, I, 8-9. In contrasting the good Melvil with the evil Fathom, Smollett
was also following Fielding's comparison of Tom Jones with Blifil, a pattern in-
creasingly popular with educational theorists like Thomas Day in his *Sanford and
Merton* and ultimately accepted by Jane Austen. The French translator of Smollett's
novel recognized this pattern and entitled his translation *Fathom et Melvil*.

[6] English and Hungarian customs are compared but once (*Fathom*, I, 40).

[7] *Ibid.*, pp. 124-38; see also p. 143.   [8] *Ibid.*, II, 1-21.

using a device already followed in *Roderick Random* and *Peregrine Pickle*. Having exhausted the potentialities for humor of the Paris group, Smollett introduces Sir Stentor Stile, the blustering, sharping Englishman who dresses in the accepted mode of an English jockey, not, as he boasts, because of a wager, but in order to disguise his intentions as a gambler. If Sir Stentor is not drawn from life, he certainly owes his origin to Smollett's ingrained prejudice against the prevalence of French fashions in English life.[9] Although Smollett may not have admired Sir Stentor's mode of gaining a livelihood, he did relish his mode of attack.

By all odds the most colorful chapters in *Fathom*, not only because they are welcomed as an escape from the tedious history of the "Noble Castalian" but also because they are animated, are those given over to Fathom's stagecoach journey from Deal to London. In them Smollett describes a foreigner's first impressions of England. All subjects are touched upon—the countryside, the indifference or open hostility of the natives, the roughness of English humor, and the stupidity of officials—and through it all is woven the story of Fathom's deception of the "fair Elenor."[10] It is a masterly description of subjects upon which Smollett had made many firsthand observations, and the accuracy of which is attested by several foreign travelers, notably Joseph Baretti's story of his journey from London to the coast for the purpose of embarking for Spain.[11] Fathom is greeted in London by his old accomplice Ratchcali,[12] whose delineation of the English people is as caustic and trenchant as any of the characterizations of the French in the *Travels*. Fathom immediately poses as a foreign art connoisseur, a role in which he plays upon the credulity of the English; but, having exposed the reception accorded him as a foreigner of rank by the polite society of London, Fathom drops his foreign pose and becomes little more than a needy English adventurer, differing little from

[9] See, e.g., *Travels*, pp. 52–54, and *Fathom*, I, 139–48.

[10] *Fathom*, I, 180–205; cf. also II, 81, 107.

[11] *A Journey from London to Genoa* (London, 1770), I, 3–13.

[12] *Fathom*, I, 202–4.

Roderick or Peregrine except in his villainy. Again, as in *Peregrine*, at the turning-point in the story when Fathom's fortune ebbs and the tide begins to run against him, Smollett steps aside and justifies his design in these words:

> Perfidious wretch! thy crimes turn out so atrocious, that I half repent me of having undertaken to record thy memoirs; yet such monsters ought to be exhibited to public view, that mankind may be upon their guard against imposture; that the world may see how fraud is apt to overshoot itself; and that, as virtue, though it may suffer for a while, will triumph in the end; so iniquity, though it may prosper for a season, will at last be overtaken by that punishment and disgrace which are its due.[13]

In short, the last third of *Ferdinand Count Fathom* corresponds to the last act of a drama wherein, to adopt Smollett's language, "the clue of the labyrinth" is unwound, the villain gets his due, and the supremacy of good over evil is re-established.

The discouraging reception of *Ferdinand Count Fathom* turned Smollett from prose fiction; not until 1760—seven years later—did he embark on a fourth novel, *Sir Launcelot Greaves*. As one of the projectors and licensees, he had helped launch in 1760 the new *British Magazine*, and with the desire to make an initial contribution in his most acceptable vein, he wrote *Sir Launcelot Greaves*, this time imitating *Don Quixote*, a translation of which he had completed five years earlier. The opening instalment of *Sir Launcelot* appeared in the first issue (January, 1760), and the novel was continued a chapter a month for two years. Six months after he launched the story, Smollett was in Scotland, where he received, as will be pointed out, the honor of election to the guild of the Edinburgh corporation, and where he was the guest of George Home at Paxton in Berwickshire.[14] According to Scott, whenever the time for the post drew near, Smollett would hastily compose another chapter of the novel and dispatch it to London. Whether this urgent, last-minute mode of composition persisted during the ensuing eighteen months is not known, but the complete novel bears traces of haste and interruptions, especially in the characters of Crabshaw and Dolly

---

[13] *Ibid.*, II, 87. [14] Scott, *Works*, III, 107.

Cowslip, whose dialect, for example, varies from broad Yorkshire to witty, conventional English repartee.

The story opens with one of Smollett's greatest scenes—
the first of its kind in English fiction—when, without the conventional preamble of a biographer or historian, he plunges
in medias res, introducing Fillet, Captain Crowe, Tom Clarke,
and Ferret at their chance encounter before the fire of the
Black Lion Inn on the "great northern road from York to
London"—not a fictitious inn but the famous Black Lion at
Weston near Sutton-on-the-Trent and Scarthing Moor, in
Nottinghamshire.[15] Settled for the evening in friendly dis-
course, the travelers are startled by the arrival of Sir Launcelot Greaves of Greavesbury Hall, near Ashenton in the West
Riding of Yorkshire, but they see only enough of him to
arouse their curiosity; and, after he retires, they press Tom
Clarke, an acquaintance, to tell them of this strange figure.
Tom, like a picaro servant, unfolds the story of Sir Launcelot's birth, his education, and his troubles with his neighbors,
the Darnels; and, once he has concluded his tale, the traditional picaresque plot of the novel is under way.[16]

Some perception of Smollett's method is gained by the
discovery that, in addition to Weston, other localities and
scenes can be traced on contemporary maps and that two of
the proper names may have a basis in fact. In Smollett's
time there was, as mentioned in the novel, an Ashenton in
the hundred of Stafford, West Riding, Yorkshire. Ashenton
was the seat of the D'Arceys, of whom Sir Conyers sat in
Parliament from 1754 until his death in 1759; but what relation the fictitious Darnels of Ashenton had to the D'Arceys of
Ashenton, other than a similarity in names, has not been discovered. Near by Ashenton, in the same hundred, was a
Gravesburgh or Greasburg, as it is variously given, which

[15] Charles G. Harper, *The Great North Road* (London, 1901), I, 253–54.

[16] Smollett's critical understanding of picaresque literature increased with the
years. In January, 1763, subsequent to the composition of *Sir Launcelot Greaves,*
there appeared in the *Critical Review* (XV, 13–21) an article which, though unsigned,
appears to be from Smollett's pen and which contains some remarkably acute observations on the genre. The passage is too long to quote here, but it should be consulted by all students of Smollett and the picaresque novel.

supplied the name at least of the hero. As recorded in the
novel, Weston is ninety miles through Sheffield and Ferry-
bridge from Greasburg. From Weston, Sir Launcelot and
Crabshaw pursue their way toward London and shortly afterward run afoul of some local authorities in a small borough.
It is probable that the particular borough in which they become involved in the law was West Retford in Nottinghamshire, a village like the one in the novel boasting of a White
Hart Inn and situated on the road from Weston to Bugden.
From West Retford, Captain Crowe could easily make a
short excursion in the direction of Birmingham and return
to the main London road in time to be rescued from the angry
farmers by Sir Launcelot and Tom Clarke; but the location
of the inn at the Sign of St. George of Cappadocia, to which
they retreated, has not been discovered. The journey finally
carries the little party through Bugden, Hatfield, and on to
the Bull and Gate Inn, Holborn. Before entering London,
Captain Crowe recommends to Sir Launcelot as a pleasant
place "a special good upper deck hard by St. Catherine's in
Wapping"; Sir Launcelot instead puts up in a small house
near Golden Square. Once settled in lodgings, Sir Launcelot,
in the continued pursuit of his beloved Aurelia Darnel, visits
the prisons and in particular the King's Bench prison in St.
George's Field. He is later confined in an insane asylum, from
which he is eventually rescued; but, wherever he goes or
whatever he sees, he still remains a Yorkshire gentleman, a
stranger in London. His travels and adventures are fittingly
concluded by his happy union with Aurelia and their return
to Yorkshire.

It is apparent that in the composition of *Sir Launcelot*
Smollett again resorted to his own travel experiences. The
description of the Black Lion at Weston, the localization of
the opening of the novel in the West Riding—these and many
more scenes undoubtedly grew out of Smollett's recollections
of his journey to Scotland in 1750 or 1753. If chapter vii and
following were, as Scott asserts, written after June, 1760, then
Smollett may have been drawing on almost daily experiences

when he described the borough election, Justice Gobble holding court, Dolly Cowslip with her Yorkshire dialect, and the various inns, including the Sign of St. George of Cappadocia. Obviously, the long account of the King's Bench prison was included, because Smollett, as an outcome of the suit of Admiral Knowles, had recently been confined there from November 28, 1760, to February 28, 1761. On several occasions Smollett and his family found quarters in Golden Square, and later he has the Brambles of *Humphry Clinker* lodge in the same vicinage. No evidence has as yet been found that Smollett had in mind any tenant of Greasburg Hall or a member of the D'Arcey family when he created Sir Launcelot and the Darnels. Captain Crowe is another of Smollett's seamen stranded ashore, but Ferret is a rather close and not entirely unsympathetic portrait of Smollett's old rival Shebbeare.[17]

Whether *Sir Launcelot Greaves* is better conceived and executed than *Ferdinand Count Fathom* may be questioned. The great fault in the novel is Smollett's unimaginative and almost slavish imitation of Don Quixote in the character of Sir Launcelot. Smollett fails to translate the knight into terms of English life or an English squire; he carries over ineptly all the anachronisms of knight-errantry—the armor, vigils, combats, and the like, which are well motivated and appropriate in sixteenth-century Spain but not in eighteenth-century England. But once the original blunder of adhering too closely to Cervantes is accepted or discounted—a blunder for which Smollett attempted a rather lame excuse[18]— there remains much that is excellent in the novel. More extensively and with happier results than in *Fathom*, Smollett has caught some of Fielding's detached point of view, his leisurely rich style, and his fondness for burlesque. Best of all are the many scenes of rural English life for which both Fielding and Smollett are famous; indeed, a careful reading of *Sir Launcelot Greaves*, *Joseph Andrews*, and *Pickwick Papers* will reveal

---

[17] Foster, "Smollett's Pamphleteering Foe Shebbeare," *Publications of the Modern Language Association*, LVII, 1053–54, 1096–1100.

[18] *Sir Launcelot Greaves*, pp. 16–17.

that these three novels have more in common than is generally appreciated.

As an experiment in prose fiction, however, *Sir Launcelot Greaves* is most important in Smollett's development as a novelist. Some of the rawness and buffoonery of Smollett's early humor is still present, but there is also a foretaste of the mellow tone, the genial humor, the rich and original delineation of English life in *Humphry Clinker*.

CHAPTER VI

THE YEARS OF SEDENTARY TOIL
IN LONDON

IN THE summer of 1750 Smollett established himself in
Monmouth House, Chelsea, where he resided for the ensuing thirteen years. Ostensibly he had not as yet abandoned his profession, for in June, 1750, he journeyed to Aberdeen to receive a medical degree from Marischal College;[1]
but, as the decade advanced, he engaged more and more in
journalistic enterprises. Quantitatively, these thirteen years
were by all odds Smollett's most productive period, but he
toiled for his generation and not posterity. Resolutely in a
hostile English London he made his way with his pen until
he won recognition as a translator, editor, critic, and historian. As a journalist he all but sold himself to the printers, and
at the end of his labors he was an embittered and broken
man.

A chronological survey of this crowded and confused period
in Smollett's life does not fall within the scope of the present
study. Only three subjects are of immediate interest in these
thirteen years: first, Smollett's travels; second, his residence
in London as an alien Scot; and, third, his contacts as a journalist with the literature of travel. Even at the expense of
some repetition in chronology, it seems best to take up each
of these topics separately.

Although his commitments to publishers confined him

---

[1] Smollett's entry lacks the customary record, attestations, and comments noted
in the record when the degree was granted *in absentia* (Peter John Anderson [ed.],
Fasti Academiae Mariscallanae Aberdonensis [Aberdeen, 1889–98], II, 116). In his
Travels (p. 113) Smollett alludes to a rapid journey of two hundred miles, which
may have been this visit to Scotland.

rather closely to London, Smollett escaped now and then to Bath from the long and irksome hours in his study. By 1753 his increasing fame had spread to Scotland, and the town council of Edinburgh "Appointed the Dean of Gild and his Councill to admitt and receive Tobias Smollett Esquire Physician in London to be Burges and Gild brother in the most ample form," but Smollett failed to appear in person, and the admission lapsed or was forgotten.[2] Smollett, like many Scots, was "endowed with some share of that affectionate prejudice in favour of his relations and countrymen, of which the natives of Scotland are accused by their philosophic neighbours,"[3] and by 1753 he could no longer resist the desire to visit his home and friends in Scotland. He had gone out into the world an obscure young man of scarcely nineteen years, and now he returned, fifteen years later, a widely traveled and successful Scot.

Smollett's fame had preceded him among his family and his friends, and he found a warm and hearty reception awaiting him. He renewed contacts with his family, particularly his cousin, James Smollett of Bonhill, to whom he later addressed an interesting letter on the origin and meaning of the family name. Dr. Moore's account of the familiar scene when Smollett was greeted by his mother is one of the most pleasant glimpses of Smollett in his family life:

> With the connivance of Mrs. Telfer [his sister], on his arrival, he was introduced to his mother as a gentleman from the West Indies, who was intimately acquainted with her son. The better to support his assumed character he endeavoured to preserve a very serious countenance, approaching to a frown; but while the old lady's eyes were riveted with a kind of wild and eager stare on his countenance, he could not refrain from smiling. She immediately sprung from her chair, and throwing her arms around his neck, exclaimed, "Ah, my son! my son! I have found you at last!"

[2] For full transcripts of the notices relating to Smollett in the Register of Burgesses and Guild Brethren in Edinburgh and for the interpretation of these notices, I am indebted to Charles B. Boog Watson. For the abbreviated entries on Smollett see Charles B. Boog Watson, *Roll of Edinburgh Burgess and Guild-Brethren, 1701–1760* ("Scottish Record Society," Part 112 [Edinburgh, 1929]), p. 189. *The Burgesses & Guild Brethren of Glasgow, 1751–1846,* ed. James R. Anderson ("Scottish Record Society," Part 116 [Edinburgh, 1931–35]), does not contain Smollett's name.

[3] Moore, *Life,* p. 103.

She afterwards told him, that if he had kept his austere look, and continued to *gloom*, he might have escaped detection some time longer; but your old roguish smile, added she, betrayed you at once.[4]

Nor was he forgotten by his friends, partly because his fame had reflected some glory on Scotland, partly because his family was prominent in Scottish life, but chiefly because he had been generous and hospitable to countrymen in London. In Musselburgh he was the guest of Dr. Alexander Carlyle, who introduced him to several of his friends there, and again in Edinburgh. Dr. Moore, who knew Smollett when he was in Paris in 1750, entertained him in Glasgow, where Smollett visited the familiar scenes of his apprenticeship and university life. He also traveled extensively in Scotland, but he found every object "shrunk in its dimensions." "When the memory," he confessed later in his *Travels*, "is not very correct, the imagination always betrays her into such extravagances. When I first revisited my own country, after an absence of fifteen years, I found everything diminished . . . . and I could scarce believe my own eyes."[5]

After the visit of 1753 to Scotland, Smollett returned refreshed and strengthened to London, there to pass the ten most arduous years of his life. During this period he published a translation of *Don Quixote*, supervised the compilation of a seven-volume compendium of voyages, edited the *Critical Review*, wrote the *Briton* to support the administration of the Earl of Bute, founded and contributed to the *British Magazine*, prepared a nine-volume history of England, and completed two novels—to name only the better known of his works. Confining as were his manifold journalistic labors, he nevertheless found time for a short trip to Flushing in 1759,[6] and in July of the following year he was in Scotland, where he was the guest of George Home at Paxton in Berwickshire. On the occasion of this visit to Scotland,[7] the town

4 "The particulars of the interview I had from Lieut. Colonel [Alexander] Smollett, Member of Parliament for the Shire of Dumbarton, and son to Mr. Smollett of Bonhill" (Moore, *Life*, pp. 103-4). Cf. *Humphry Clinker*, II, 113-16, and Chambers, *Smollett*, p. 164.

5 *Travels*, p. 48.

6 *Ibid.*, p. 4, and *Letters*, p. 63.   7 Scott, *Works*, III, 107.

council of Edinburgh admitted him once again to the honors of the corporation, and on July 30 the following entry was made in the Register of Burgesses and Guild Brethren of Edinburgh:

> Tobias Smollett Esq: Doctor of Medicine compearing is made Burges and Gild brother of this burgh for the good services done by him to the interest thereof conform to an act of the Town Council of the date of these presents Likeas the Dean of Gild and his Council conform to the said act Declare the said Tobias Smollett his admission as valid Effectual and Sufficient as if he had paid the whole dues in use to be paid by Unfreemen And gave his Oath &c.[8]

The honor was more then complimentary; it carried with it all the rights and privileges customarily granted only upon the full payment of the fee or duty.

The same year he "made some advances towards the Consulship of Madrid"[9] but was offered instead the consulate at Nice, which he did not accept because the "appointments" were insufficient to maintain his family.[10] By the spring of 1762 his health began to break under the long and confining hours imposed on him by his many undertakings, and he was compelled again to seek recuperation in travel.

At first he took short excursions in England. Of these trips he wrote Dr. Moore in October, 1762:

> Your last found me in the country,[11] to which I had retired for the benefit of a purer air; but whether it was too keen for my lungs, or the change of bed produced a fresh cold, I was driven home by the asthma; and soon after I went to Dover with a view to bathe in the sea, and to use the exercise of riding on horseback and sailing in a vessel alternately. There, too, I was disappointed. Immediately after my arrival the weather broke; my asthma returned; my flesh fell away, and my spirits faded; so that I returned very disconsolate, and almost despairing of relief. The journey, however, did me service. I have been at home these eight days, and find myself better than I have been these three years. Indeed, I am

[8] See n. 2 above.

[9] Noyes (*Letters*, pp. 63, 187 n.) sees a reference to this in a letter, October 30, 1759, in which Smollett writes to Dr. Macaulay, "I long to know what steps you have taken with respect to Spain."

[10] *Letters*, p. 79.

[11] Smollett may have been referring to this excursion when he wrote in the *Travels* (p. 34), "While I stayed at Hastings, for the conveniency of bathing."

at present perfectly well; but how long I shall enjoy this respite I cannot forsee.[12]

In the same letter he goes on to express the hope that in the spring he may "be able to make an excursion to the south of France" and confesses his disappointment in a scheme to go as a physician "to our army in Portugal." The relief he found in the visit to Dover in the summer of 1762 was not permanent. On October 2, after a journey from Southampton through New Forest,[13] he visited Bath without recovering his health.[14] After Christmas he was back in Chelsea, conscious more than ever that he must quit England for a milder climate.[15] At this juncture he wrote John Home, secretary to the Earl of Bute, the prime minister, seeking the consulship at Madrid or Marseille, the latter being then vacant. He received neither. In six months he was on his way to the south of France, with little assurance that he would ever again see his friends in London and Scotland.

Smollett's recreation in travel between 1750 and 1763 had far less influence upon his writings than did his residence in England as an alien Scot. English animosity toward the Scots was no new thing in the eighteenth century, but between 1760 and 1763 it reached the pitch of a national phobia. While Smollett was one of the public victims of this particular outbreak of racial antagonism, he experienced it in varying degrees all his life. If *Roderick Random* gives any autobiographical insight into Smollett's first contact with the English, it makes it abundantly clear that Smollett at the outset was made acutely aware of his racial origins. From the first day he tramped the streets of London through all his travels and years of labor in London, Smollett apparently neither was allowed, nor wished, to forget that he was Scottish.

As early as 1740 he encountered the prejudice against Scotland when he solicited the producers with his tragedy, *The Regicide*. During the Jacobite Rebellion of 1745 he was

[12] Noyes, "Another Smollett Letter," *Modern Language Notes*, XLII (April, 1927), 231-35.

[13] *Letters*, pp. 77-78.   [14] *Travels*, p. 2.   [15] *Letters*, pp. 78-79.

in London on Black Wednesday when the Highlanders were at Derby and again later when the first news of the Battle of Culloden arrived. Dr. Carlyle, who was in his company, recounts how they had to skulk home from a Scottish coffeehouse through alleys with their swords in their hands, fearful to speak lest their Scottish burr betray them. Later, while in the company of some friends, Smollett heard the fuller accounts of the victory telling of the cruelties of the Duke of Cumberland in slaying the wounded. His indignation would brook no delay; withdrawing from the company, he sat down and wrote in a short time, in what is remembered as his best poem, his passionate protest, "The Tears of Scotland."

> Mourn, hapless Caledonia, mourn
> Thy banish'd peace, thy laurels torn!
> Thy sons, for valour long renown'd,
> Lie slaughter'd on their native ground;
> Thy hospitable roofs no more
> Invite the stranger to the door;
> In smoky ruins sunk they lie
> The monuments of cruelty
>
> . . . .
>
> While the warm blood bedews my veins,
> And unimpair'd remembrance reigns,
> Resentment of my country's fate
> Within my filial breast shall beat;
> And, spite of her insulting foe,
> My sympathizing verse shall flow:
> "Mourn, hapless Caledonia, mourn
> Thy banish'd peace, thy laurels torn."[16]

The effectual suppression of the Rebellion of 1745 might have terminated the English dislike of the Scots had not the Union opened to the Scots a rich and expanding field for professional and commercial activity which they eagerly exploited, but their immediate and notable achievements, their pride and clannishness, effectually aroused the English in protest and antagonism.[17] When Smollett launched the *Critical Review* in 1756, he received almost immediately the full blast

[16] William Richardson, *Poems and Plays* (Edinburgh, 1805), I, 124–25.

[17] For a general discussion of the effect upon literature see Henry Grey Graham, *Scottish Men of Letters in the Eighteenth Century* (London, 1901), chap. xi.

of Shebbeare's *The Occasional Critic, or the Decrees of the Scotch Tribunal* (1757), in which he and his associate editors were condemned for ignorance and stupidity, but most emphatically for the worst stigma of all—their supposed Scottish origins.[18] The attack was continued in Reed's *A Sop in the Pan for a Physical Critic* (1759), the anonymous *Battle of the Reviews* (1760), and other similar pamphlets, and eventually in a doggerel called "Queries to the Critical Reviewers" (1763):

> Ye judging Caledonian Pedlars,
>   That to a scribling world give law,
> Laid up engarretted, like medlars,
>   Ripening to rottenness in straw.
>
> . . . .
>
> Why d'ye suppose that the sublime
>   Should only rant beneath Scotch bonnets?
> Why humour, wit, poetic rhime
>   Be only found in Scottish sonnets?[19]

In spite of opposition and open antagonism, the Scots gradually made headway in London and prospered in all walks of life. In 1760 George III ascended the throne and, besides showing marked favoritism for his guardian Lord Bute, who was a Scot, a Stuart, and a descendant of the Jacobites, assisted rather than opposed the influx of Scottish office-seekers. Meanwhile English anger against the failure of Bute and the incapacity of the king, as well as the mutual dislikes of Whig and Tory, found vent, not in political discussions or tirades, but in a thoroughgoing slandering of the Scots. The popular press enlisted the talents of such journalists as Wilkes, Churchill, and Lloyd and of such artists as Paul Sandby, Gravelot, M. Darling, Thomas Patch, John Collet, W. H. Bunbury, and the great caricaturist, Lord

---

[18] *Letters*, pp. 149–50; see also *Critical Review*, IV (October, 1757), 332, 338. With reference to Shebbeare's pamphlet Smollett wrote to Dr. Moore: "The authors of the Critical Review have been insulted & abused as a *Scotch Tribunal*. The Truth is, there is no Author so wretched, but he will meet with countenance in England, if he attacks our nation in any shape. You cannot conceive the Jealousy that prevails against us. Nevertheless it is better to be envied than despised" (*Letters*, p. 51).

[19] *The Political Controversy: or Weekly Magazine*, III (March 7, 1763), 284–85.

Townshend. Against these and in defense of the Tory government and the Scottish people were arrayed Smollett, Murphy,
and Hogarth. Wilkes gathered into the pages of the *North
Briton* and Churchill into "The Prophecy of Famine"[20] all the
traditional abuse of the Scots, together with the antagonism
generated by the acts of the government or by the de-
fenses and satires of Smollett and Hogarth. Little is to be
gained by enlarging upon these past animosities or reviewing
the sorry parade of journalistic disparagement of the Scots
in the many popular prints and broadsides;[21] yet it should be
emphasized that the prejudices reflected in these writings
were nowise confined to the London mobs and political writers; they penetrated to all classes. Johnson's frequent thrusts
were only the humorous commonplaces of everyday prejudice
and are too well known to need repeating.[22] After Smollett
rescued Johnson's servant, Francis Barber, from the press-
gang, "Dr. Johnson always spoke of Dr. Smollett thereafter
with great respect:—'A scholarly man, sir, although a
Scot.' "[23] Horace Walpole gradually became more acrimoni-
ous in his references to the Scots as the years advanced, until
in 1773 he scorned the name of Briton since it implied Scotland;[24] by 1780 he had reached the point where he exclaimed :

But what a nation is Scotland; in every reign engendering traitors to
the state, and false and pernicious to the kings that favour it the most!
National prejudices, I know, are very vulgar; but, if there are national
characteristics, can one but dislike the soils and climate that concur to
produce them?[25]

[20] *The Poetical Works of Charles Churchill*, ed. W. Tooke (London, 1892). For
Smollett see I, 61, 65, 68, 74, 106; II, 5, 10.

[21] For collections see *The Political Controversy* (5 vols.; London, 1762–63);
Gisbal, an Hyperborean Tale (2d ed.; London, 1762); *The British Antidote to Cale-
donian Poison* (2 vols.; 5th ed.; London, [1763, 1764]); J. Pridden, *The Scots Scourge*
(2 vols.; 3d ed.; London, 1764); and F. G. Stephens, *Catalogue of Prints and Drawings in the British Museum, Division I: Political and Personal Satires* (London,
1870–83), IV, lxxii–lxxxi.

[22] *Boswell's Life of Johnson*, ed. George Birkbeck Hill (New York, 1891), VI,
289–323, "Dicta Philosophi."

[23] Oliphant Smeaton, *Tobias Smollett* ("Famous Scots Series" [Edinburgh and
London, 1897]), p. 94.

[24] *The Letters of Horace Walpole*, ed. Mrs. Paget Toynbee (Oxford, 1903), VIII,
244.

[25] *Ibid.*, XI, 222.

In the Preface to his letters Junius also lashed the Scots for their characteristic prudence, selfish nationalism, indefatigable smile, perservering assiduity, and everlasting profession of discreet and moderate resentment, and in the letters themselves he continued the attack on their treachery.[26] After Scotsmen had suffered two generations of abuse, it is little wonder that Wendeborn, the German traveler, should write in 1791: "It is, likewise, rather curious, that the English, who pride themselves on the name of Britons, which they bear in common with the Scotch, are, notwithstanding, rather more averse to them, than even to a foreigner."[27]

Smollett, second only to Lord Bute, received the brunt of the attack, especially in his capacity as official journalist of the administration and, according to his enemies, as "the paid Scottish advocate of Scotchmen." As early as 1760, two years before the *Briton*, he appeared with Lord Bute in a derogatory print called "Sawney Discovered or the Scotch Intrudors,"[28] the purpose of which was to disclose Bute's secret influence over the Princess of Wales and his determination to fill all offices with Scotsmen. It caricatures Smollett in the habit of a Scottish doctor crying, with an apparent desire to be of assistance, "I'll shew my great talent." With the appearance of the first issue of the *Briton*, his troubles began in earnest. In May there was circulated a print entitled "The Mountebank"[29] in which Lord Bute as a quack doctor makes his speech in broad Scotch, and Smollett in a long plaid dressing gown, fool's cap, hornbook in girdle, and the *Briton* under his arm, plays the role of Bute's zany. Shortly afterward Smollett figured again in "The Fishermen,"[30] along with Murphy, Churchill, and Beardmore, who are represented as angling in the "Waters of Sedition." Here he is wearing

---

[26] *Junius*, ed. John Wade (London, 1850), I, 98–99; see also I, 264–65, 307, 330–31.

[27] F. A. Wendeborn, *A View of England towards the Close of the Eighteenth Century* (London, 1791), I, 374.

[28] Stephens, *Catalogue of Prints and Drawings*, IV, No. 3825. See also No. 3844, "The Hungry Mob of Scriblers and Etchers," which delineates the hirelings employed by Lord Bute. Smollett is not clearly caricatured in the group.

[29] *Ibid.*, No. 3853.   [30] *Ibid.*, No. 3876.

plaids, and from his actions, as well as from the remarks of his fellows, one gathers that he is heartily sick of his task. Before the satirists were through with him, he was represented as completely defeated, the triumphant foot of John Wilkes resting on his neck.[31] He appeared in approximately twenty-two extant satiric prints;[32] no wonder, then, that he felt "traduced by malice, persecuted by faction, abandoned by false patrons"[33] when he sailed for France in June, 1763.

In the present state of Smollett's biography, it is difficult to estimate the effect of English antipathy upon his life and works. In his public utterances on the whole he maintained a passive attitude. One or two brief asides in the novels may have offended English patriotism, as, for example, Roderick's encounter in a coffee-house with a testy old Tory "who contradicted everything that was advanced in favour of his Most Christian Majesty, with a surliness truly English,"[34] or Matthew Bramble's several reflections on "Old English hospitality" in *Humphry Clinker*. In public his abiding desire and care was to mitigate and correct the rage of the English, both as a journalist in the *Briton* and later as a novelist in *Humphry Clinker*, which in part he wrote consciously, not in the spirit but in the words of Horace Walpole, "to vindicate the Scots." Among his most intimate friends he may have been more outspoken, if one is to judge by a comment in one of his letters when he stigmatized England as "a land where felicity is held to consist in stupefying port and overgrown buttocks of beef, where genius is lost and taste extinguished."[35]

Unquestionably, however, English antagonism increased the odds against which Smollett struggled to make a hard-won living. To that extent it undoubtedly embittered him and provoked him to an occasional misanthropic outburst. On the whole, his resentment was not chronic, for at the time

[31] *Ibid.*, Nos. 4028 and 3027.

[32] *Ibid.*, Nos. 3825, 3866, 3867, 3876, 3877, 3887, 3890, 3909, 3910, 3914, 3916, 3917, 3941, 3956, 3958, 3966, 3971, 3975, 3986, 4028, 4037, and 4061.

[33] *Travels*, p. 1.

[34] *Roderick Random*, II, 195.   [35] *Letters*, pp. 29 and 139.

the editorship of the *Briton* was calling down on his head the thunders of Wilkes and Churchill, he still wrote calmly:

My difficulties have arisen from my own indiscretion; from a warm temper easily provoked to rashness; from a want of courage to refuse that which I cannot grant without doing injustice to my own family; from indolence, bashfulness and want of economy. I am sensible of all my weaknesses; I have suffered by them severely; but I have not vigour of mind sufficient to reform; and so I must go on at the old rate to the end of the chapter.[36]

Thus, while he appears to have been actuated neither by the great passion for literary fame that inspired David Hume nor by the conceit of John Home that thirsted for flattery and acclaim, he valued the human bonds of friendship and loyalty more than all else:

I envy no man of merit; and I can safely say I do not even repine at the success of those who have no merit. I am old enough to have seen and observed that we are all playthings of fortune and that it depends upon something as insignificant and precarious as the tossing up of a halfpenny, whether a man rises to affluence and honours, or continues to his dying day struggling with the difficulties and disgraces of life. I desire to live quietly with all mankind, and, if possible, to be upon good terms with all those who have distinguished themselves by their merit.[37]

It is precisely because friendship was so prized by Smollett that the gulf that divided Scot from Englishman touched Smollett in his private life, and this barrier in turn left its mark on his prose fiction. The racial animosity of the London English isolated Smollett and tended to restrict his social life to the company of Scots. Of course, lines were not so sharply drawn as to exclude him from the acquaintance of all Englishmen, yet habitually he met and conversed with them as if they were of another race, and he resided in their midst as an alien. London he knew from long residence, but it was the London of public life—coffee-houses, ordinaries, gaming-rooms, prisons, theaters, public gardens. Of the citizens, he knew the mobs in the streets, the petty criminals, the small merchants such as Gamaliel Pickle, and some public figures, but with the educated, cultivated, or titled Englishmen he

[36] Noyes, "Another Smollett Letter," *Modern Language Notes*, XLII, 232.

[37] *Letters*, pp. 69–70.

had a limited acquaintance. Like Smollett, the young men in his novels are strangers in London, moving through a series of adventures that befall strangers or travelers.

Because of the barrier of racial hatred, however, Smollett cherished the friendship of the Scots in London all the more warmly. Almost all that is known of his private life with friends in London consists of the glimpses we get of his leisure hours with the small circle of successful Scottish physicians, merchants, and authors—all like himself hardy adventurers in an unfriendly city. Acquaintances from Scotland often paid him a visit, or needy Scots sought him out for advice and financial help. On Sunday afternoons he kept open house to a motley crowd of indigent or eccentric men of all races;[38] otherwise, many of his leisure hours outside his home were passed, as might be expected, in the several coffee-houses in the neighborhood of Charing Cross where Scots gathered. The coffee-houses patronized by the Scots appear to have been grouped together on Charing Cross and Cockspur Street; in three of these Smollett was a familiar figure. It is this circumscribed life in the colony of his own nation that demonstrates how much Smollett was a foreigner and a stranger in London, why he never ceased to be a Scot proud of his own race and culture, and it explains why to this day he has possessed a definite foreign flavor for most English readers.

The Golden Ball[39] in the corner of Cockspur Street catered to adventurers fresh from the north when their finances were low. Here Dr. Carlyle often met with Blair, Smith, and Smollett for a "frugal supper and a little punch," when they were regaled "by Smollett's agreeable stories, which he told with peculiar grace." Here, too, Carlyle and Smollett received the news of Culloden and crept home through alleys to escape detection by the London mobs.[40]

---

[38] *Humphry Clinker*, I, 162–74.

[39] J. Paul de Castro, "Principal London Coffee-Houses, Taverns, and Inns in the Eighteenth Century," *Notes and Queries, Twelfth Series*, VI (April 3, 1920), 85.

[40] Carlyle, *Autobiography*, pp. 189–90.

Forrest's,[41] another Scottish coffee-house, was situated opposite the Mews Gate, Charing Cross, and there also, according to the observations of Ali Mohammed Hadgi, the conversation turned chiefly on places and pensions.[42] It was in operation as early as March 15, 1742.[43] To Forrest's came John Cathcart, a Scot, the director of the hospitals of the West Indies expeditions (including Carthagena), and from it in 1744 were dated his three letters of defense against Admiral Vernon's charge of mismanagement in the Cuban expedition.[44] Again, however, the fullest record of Smollett's association with Forrest's is from Dr. Carlyle, who on a memorable occasion in 1759 with Home and Robertson dined with Smollett. At this time Smollett was residing in Chelsea, coming in once a week to Forrest's to meet the drudges who were engaged in his hackwork ventures. One evening two of them were invited to join the party at supper, and, as Smollett expected, they amused the company, "for they were curious characters."[45]

Above all other London coffee-houses of Smollett's day, that known as the "British"[46] was the London club of Scots. It was situated in Cockspur Street, almost opposite the Cannon Coffee-House and adjoining the Court of Requests. By 1714 it had already gained a reputation as the place of general resort for Scots.[47] Carlyle went there on all his visits to the capital. As a young man in London in 1746, fresh from his medical studies at Leiden, he was lonely until he heard of the

---

[41] De Castro, "Principal London Coffee-Houses," *Notes and Queries, Twelfth Series*, VII (July 24, 1920), 68.

[42] Anthony Hilliar, *A Brief and Merry History of Great Britain* (London, [1740]), p. 22.

[43] *Daily Advertiser*, March 15, 1742, and *Connoisseur*, No. I (January 31, 1755), p. 8.

[44] John Cathcart, *A Letter to the Honourable Edward Vernon* (London, 1744), pp. 4, 11, 12, 13.

[45] Carlyle, *Autobiography*, p. 339.

[46] De Castro, "Principal London Coffee-Houses," *Notes and Queries, Twelfth Series*, VI (February, 1920), 31; VII (July 17, 1920), 50–51. There were two coffee-houses called the "British"; the other and less famous was in the Old Palace Yard.

[47] [John Macky], *A Journey through England* (London, 1714), p. 108.

British Coffee-House and there found many of his old friends from Scotland, was introduced to Smollett,[48] and met Captain Cheap, recently returned from the wreck of the "Wager" on the coast of Chile. "Captain Cheap," Carlyle writes, "had a predilection for his countrymen" and had come down to the British to inquire about Guthrie as a possible writer-editor for Anson's voyage. The tavern where, on a memorable evening, Smollett wrote the "Tears of Scotland" remains unidentified, but surely such an outspoken testimony of Scottish loyalty may well have been composed in one of these coffee-houses, either Forrest's or the British.[49] The latter early acquired social prestige, and in 1750 the Duke of Bedford was able to summon all sixteen of the Scottish peers by letters sent under one cover to the British Coffee-House.[50] In the middle years of the century a famous club of Scottish physicians met once a week at eight in the evening at the British Coffee-House, among whom were Pitcairn, Armstrong, Orme, Dickson, William Hunter, Clephane, and Graham of Pall Mall. Alexander Carlyle, who supplies this information, gives the names of seven members of the club and indicates that there were others, but his failure to include the name of Smollett makes Smollett's membership merely a subject of conjecture.[51] All of those named were his acquaintances and friends; he dined with some of them when Carlyle was their host, and he was often in their company. If he was not a member of the Scottish physicians' club, he belonged to another that had on its roster equally famous names: Wedderburn (later Lord Loughborough), Sir Harry Erskine, Robert Adams, Garrick, Douglas, Sir Gilbert Elliot, Ross Mackie, and Drs. Armstrong, Pitcairn, and William Hunter.[52]

[48] Carlyle, *Autobiography*, p. 186.

[49] Richardson, *Poems and Plays*, I, 124, 125, and Scott, *Works*, III, 187–88.

[50] Walpole, *Letters*, II, 431. See also Henry, Lord Brougham, *Lives of Men of Letters and Science, Who Flourished in the Time of George III* (London, 1845), p. 278 n., and Henry Mackenzie, *An Account of the Life and Writings of John Home* (Edinburgh, 1822), pp. 56–57.

[51] Carlyle, *Autobiography*, p. 345.   [52] Mackenzie, *Home*, pp. 56–57.

To the British Coffee-House came not only Scottish physicians, lawyers, authors, divines, and lords but also Scottish soldiers and sailors. Cheap's visits there have been mentioned. Admiral Vernon, writing to the Duke of Newcastle on December 30, 1742, recommended to his attention and good graces three Scottish captains in American regiments in the West Indies—James Mercer, Thomas Louverie, and William Hepburn, all three of whom were to be found in London at the British Coffee-House.[53] Smollett may have heard Captain Robert Mann recount his many adventures while they dined at the British.[54] There is a reasonable probability that Smollett made the acquaintance of another Scotsman, Captain Robert Stobo, at the British Coffee-House or at Forrest's. Stobo was a colonel in the Virginia militia and a captain in the Fifteenth Regiment of Foot, which landed in England in July, 1768, and immediately moved up to London.[55] It will be recalled that Captain Stobo was the person whom Smollett, in a well-known letter written some weeks later, introduced to David Hume.[56] Smollett's brief acquaintance with the Captain bore fruit in *Humphry Clinker* in the delightful character of Lismahago.

During the ministry of Lord Bute, Wilkes intimated that the British Coffee-House would be a good point of concentration for an anti-Scottish riot,[57] but the proposal was never acted upon, and the British Coffee-House continued to prosper for well over a hundred years. Robert Adam, the famous architect, designed for it a handsome façade when the house was rebuilt in 1770.[58] Boswell invited Johnson there for supper in 1772,[59] and in 1782 Lord Campbell met there once a

---

[53] Vernon, *Original Papers Relating to the Expedition to Panama* (London, 1744), p. 224.

[54] *Letters*, pp. 46 and 161; *Humphry Clinker*, II, 96.

[55] Richard Cannon, *Historical Record of the Fifteenth . . . . Regiment of Foot* (London, 1848), p. 46.

[56] *Letters*, pp. 103–4.

[57] *North Briton*, XLVI (April 30, 1763), 159.

[58] For a picture see Henry C. Shelley, *Inns and Taverns of Old London* (Boston, 1909), p. 222.

[59] *Boswell's Life of Johnson*, ed. Hill, II, 225.

week with the Beeswing Club, made up of Scotsmen. "The conversation was as good as I ever joined in," he wrote; "but the drinking was tremendous."[60]

The Golden Ball, Forrest's, and the British coffee-houses, especially Forrest's and the British, were the ones in which Smollett passed much of his leisure with countrymen in the city or in transit. Though he was thoroughly familiar with the atmosphere and the patrons, never once did he introduce any one of the three Scottish coffee-houses into his prose fiction—another clear evidence of his constant effort to avoid antagonizing English readers. He certainly visited others, probably through curiosity, either alone[61] or with Englishmen; he mentions specifically the Bedford, Moll King's,[62] the Saracen's Head, the Turk's Head, the Boar's Head, the Bear, and the Star and Garter[63]—all well-known social resorts frequented by literary figures and social lions. Yet in a century famous for clubs of all classes, especially of literary men, Smollett was never a member of any social organization save the group of Scottish physicians referred to above. No record has survived to connect his name with any of the famous clubs of his contemporaries; the tradition that he was once a guest of the Beefsteak Club may be founded upon no better evidence than the reference to the club and its gridiron in *Sir Launcelot Greaves*.[64] No other important literary figure of his day in London suffered such complete isolation from the society of playwrights, poets, novelists, critics, actors, and titled patrons.

[60] Mary Scarlett [Campbell] Hardcastle, *Life of John, Lord Campbell* (London, 1881), I, 411. For additional references to the British Coffee-House, see Lord Brougham, *Lives*, p. 278; Sir Walter Besant, *London in the Eighteenth Century* (London and New York, 1903), p. 315. After 1824 the British began to decline, and, before its demolition in 1899, it enjoyed some popularity with Americans and later with canary fanciers (*Daily Telegraph*, September 19, 1899, p. 9).

[61] Professor Knapp has called my attention to an a.l.s. by Smollett in the University of Glasgow Library dated from the "Rainbow Coffeehouse, Monday Oct. 15, 1750." Why Smollett was in this coffee-house, which was situated on Cornhill Road, is not known.

[62] *Roderick Random*, II, 207, 219; III, 15, 16.

[63] *Humphry Clinker*, I, 214, 216.

[64] Robert J. Allen, *The Clubs of Augustan London* (Cambridge, 1933), p. 144; see also pp. 165 n. and 285, and *Sir Launcelot Greaves*, pp. 40–41.

In Chelsea, on the other hand, where he resided, he was less subjected to English prejudice and participated more freely in the social life of its several coffee-houses. One of these, Don Saltero's, famous for its museum of curios rather than its food or social standing, for a hundred years or so after its founding in 1695 enjoyed the patronage and commendation of such men as Sir John Cope, Atterbury, Swift, Addison, Steele,[65] Bolingbroke, Admiral Munden (who changed plain James Salter, the proprietor, to Don Saltero), Fielding, and Ben Franklin. The only clear evidence that Smollett ever visited the museum is the presence of his name among the contributors to its collection of over 725 items, which at one time included an elf's arrow, petrified rain, the feet of a Muscovy cat, Mary Queen of Scot's pincushion, Queen Elizabeth's chambermaid's hat, a plum-pudding stone, two broad arrows of Robin Hood, and

> Monsters of all sorts . . . . :
> Strange things in nature as they grew so;
> Some relicks of the Sheba Queen,
> And fragments of the fam'd Bob Crusoe.[66]

Since the collection abounded in curios from Scotland, the West Indies, and medical science, it is hard to guess what Smollett contributed. Fifteen captains added to the collection, as well as Sir Hans Sloane (the founder), a Mr. Hunter, and Robert Mann. Pallet, the foolish artist in *Peregrine Pickle*, "would not give one corner of Saltero's coffee-house at Chelsea for all the trash" he saw in the Dutchman's famous cabinet of curios.[67] As might be supposed, the museum eventually swallowed the coffee-house, and, considering Smollett's usual squeamishness in culinary matters, it is doubtful if he met frequently with his cronies at Don Saltero's.[68]

[65] See *Tatler*, No. 34.

[66] John Timbs, *Club Life of London* (London, 1866), II, 44–48; *A Catalogue of the Rarities To Be Seen at Don Saltero's Coffee-House, in Chelsea, to Which Is Added a Complete List of the Donors Thereof*, inserted in Timbs's *Club Life*, IX, 101–10 (Widener Collection); and Alfred Beaver, *Memorials of Old Chelsea* (London, 1892), pp. 204–7.

[67] *Peregrine Pickle*, II, 208.   [68] Graham, *Scottish Men of Letters*, p. 307.

More often, and with greater pleasure, he foregathered with the "Brotherhood of the Swan," that is, in the old Swan Inn on the river bank. How many Englishmen he met here cannot be ascertained; in the only letter in which he speaks of the Swan he was writing to a Scot whom he addressed as "Dear Sawney."[69] It is quite possible, however, that the "vacant hours, among a set of honest phlegmatic Englishmen" whom he cultivated in 1754–55 in Chelsea were passed at the Swan.[70] The identities of these Englishmen remain unknown;[71] nor has it been discovered how frequently he met with them in either London or Chelsea. In relation to these scenes of pleasant social hours, there are few sadder lines in all his troubled letters than those Smollett wrote from Chelsea on December 10, 1759: "Since last May, I have hardly enjoyed one day of health; I am so subject to colds and rheums that I dare hardly stir from my own house; and shall be obliged to give all up the pleasures of society, at least those of tavern society, to which you know I have been always addicted."[72]

Because English prejudices tended to limit his social life to a small and isolated circle of Scottish friends and acquaintances, Smollett never fully identified himself with English life but remained through the years ever aware of his alien Scottish origins. Racial differences that normally would have worn off were thus kept alive, and filial loyalty to Scotland became at times in Smollett, as in many a persecuted minority, a fierce pride voiced even in the epitaph above his supposed grave near Leghorn: "Hic ossa conduntur TOBIAE SMOLLETT, Scoti."[73] When he undertook to review the years of his struggles in London, in what is perhaps the rarest of all his books, the fifth volume of his *Continuation of the Com-*

---

[69] *Letters*, p. 86.

[70] *Ibid.*, p. 33; see also *DNB*, LIII, 176.

[71] *Letters*, pp. 39 and 148-50.

[72] Knapp, "An Important Smollett Letter," *Review of English Studies*, XII (January, 1936), 77.

[73] *Plays and Poems Written by T. Smollett, M.D.* (London, 1777), p. xxiii.

plete History of England,[74] he wrote soberly and eloquently of the national prejudice of the English against the Scots that had multiplied his obstacles and embittered his life. Because the passage is little known, it is here quoted as a fitting close to a summary of Smollett's life among the English:

The jealousy of the English nation, towards their fellow-subjects on the other side of the Tweed, had discovered itself occasionally ever since the union of the crowns; and antient animosities had been kept alive by two successive rebellions which began in Scotland: but the common grudge was founded upon the success of the Scots, who had established themselves in different parts of England, and risen from very small beginnings to wealth and consideration. They had prospered in many different provinces of life, and made no contemptible figure in the cultivation of the arts and sciences. In a word, the English people looked upon them with an evil eye, as interlopers in commerce and competitors for reputation. It was not without murmuring, they had seen them aspire to the first offices in the law, the army, and the navy: but they were exasperated to find a Scot at the head of the English treasury, and the chief administration of the kingdom in his hands. These were topicks on which the writers in the opposition did not fail to expatiate. They revived, and retailed with peculiar virulence, all the calumnies, antient and modern, that ever had been uttered against the Scottish nation; some of them so gross and absurd, that they could not possibly obtain credit but among the very dregs of the people. They enlarged upon their craft, dissimulation, deceit, and national partiality. They demonstrated the dangers that threatened the interests of Old England, from the great numbers of those Northern adventurers, who had wriggled themselves into all the different departments of civil and military institution; and they insisted upon the disgrace of acquiescing under the government of a North Briton, a Stuart allied by blood to the pretender, who had expelled from court the best friends of the protestant succession, associated himself with avowed Tories, who prostituted the offices, and squandered away the wealth of England on worthless favourites of his own country. These bitter remonstrances, in which no regard was payed either to truth or decency, they reinforced with feigned circumstances, and forged lists of North Britons gratified with pensions, appointed to places, or promoted in the service; till at length the populace were incensed and impelled even to the verge of insurrection.[75]

[74] Knapp, "The Publication of Smollett's *Complete History* and *Continuation*," *Library*, XVI (December, 1935), 302–8.

[75] *Continuation of the Complete History of England* (London, 1765), V, 117–18. From a copy kindly lent by Professor Knapp.

CHAPTER VII

A JOURNALIST AND THE LITERATURE
OF TRAVEL

SMOLLETT'S career as a journalist, although it won
for him a creditable reputation among his contemporaries, has for the most part been ignored by later generations. With the possible exception of his *History of England* (4 vols., 1757–58) and the *Continuation* (5 vols., 1760–
65), his various engagements with printers were fulfilled under the pressure of manifold commitments and financial
stress and with the assistance of many a nameless hack; consequently, in vigor and originality his professional writings
do not come up to his prose fiction and are of minor value
except for biographical purposes. It was as a journalist, however, that Smollett acquired a wide knowledge of travel books
which he subsequently brought to bear on his *Travels through
France and Italy* and on *Humphry Clinker*. Without tracking
down every book that he ever read or consulted, one may,
nevertheless, grasp the range and thoroughness of his knowledge of voyages and travels by examining the subjects and
sources of some of his major journalistic undertakings.

Among the stock-in-trade of most publishers in the first
half of the eighteenth century were collections or compendi-
ums of voyages, some twenty-five of which were issued between 1690 and 1755 to satisfy a growing curiosity concerning foreign lands. To profit by this demand, Smollett signed
a contract on May 5, 1753, with Robert Dodsley, James
Rivington, and William Strahan "to complete with all convenient speed so as the whole be finished on or before the first
day of August 1754 *A New Collection of Voyages and Travels*

from the best books on these subjects extant."[1] Either the
pressure of other obligations, his conscientiousness, or the
slowness of assistants prevented Smollett from executing the
contract in the time specified. Whatever the causes, the collection did not appear until April 29, 1756,[2] when it was published anonymously in seven duodecimo volumes as *A Compendium of Authentic and Entertaining Voyages*. By the time
the *Compendium* was out, Smollett was heartily sick of the
whole undertaking and afterward never ceased to complain
of hackwork on compilations and the demands of publishers.[3]

   With the exception of the "Account of the Expedition
against Carthagena," the authorship of which Smollett acknowledged, the extent of his labors in the *Compendium* can
be estimated only on internal evidence. After sifting such
evidence, Martz, in his recent study of the *Compendium*,
ventures the somewhat vague conclusion that Smollett was
more closely "connected," to use Martz's own word, with
eight of the twenty-seven divisions than with the other nineteen. He does, however, credit Smollett with the personal
guidance of the entire compilation and the revision of the
final copy.[4] These contributions and responsibilities were
enough to give Smollett a fundamental knowledge of the
travel literature produced during the preceding two hundred
and fifty years. An even better indication, however, of his
knowledge can be found in the scope of the voyages covered
by the *Compendium* and the sources from which they were
drawn.

   According to Smollett's Preface, the *Compendium* was
unique among collections in offering a chronological survey of
world exploration:

   In the arrangement of our materials, we have deviated from the plan
   which has been followed by all other compilers of Voyages; instead of beginning with the circum-navigators, and classing together the different

[1] *Letters*, pp. 23–24.

[2] Louis L. Martz, *The Later Career of Tobias Smollett* (New Haven, 1942), p. 23.

[3] *Critical Review*, I (March, 1756), 97–106; XII (October, 1761), 237–50; and
XV (January, 1763), 42–44.

[4] See Martz, *The Later Career of Tobias Smollett*, pp. 22–29.

Voyages which have been made to the same countries; we have set out with the Discoveries of Columbus, and introduced every subsequent Voyage in chronological order, so as to form, as it were, The Annals of Navigation. Thus we trace the spirit of adventure in a regular progress thro' all the various streams of discovery, in every different channel give a new entertainment, and avoid the fatiguing sameness of immediate repetition.[5]

In conformity with the plan, Volumes I, II, and III embrace the accounts of early discoveries in the New World and the East included in almost every earlier collection. Volumes IV and V continue with six short accounts of Greenland, Iceland, and Spitsbergen, the discoveries of Nieuhoff in Brazil and the East Indies, the explorations of Baldaeus on the coast of Malabar and Coromandel and on the island of Ceylon, a description of Russia and the northern countries, the adventures of Wafer in Central America, and the "Account of the Expedition against Carthagena" by Smollett. Finally, Volumes VI and VII summarize the later circumnavigators— Dampier, Gemelli-Careri, Rogers, and Anson.

The principal sources for the twenty-seven sections of the *Compendium* were standard encyclopedic collections: *Purchas His Pilgrimes* (4 vols.; London, 1625) was drawn upon for four of the sections, the Churchills' *Collection of Voyages and Travels* (6 vols.; London, 1744–46) for thirteen, Campbell's edition of John Harris' *Navigantium atque Itinerantium Bibliotheca* (2 vols.; London, 1744–48) for nine, and Barclay's inferior *Universal Traveller* (London, 1735) for two. Frequently the major source was supplemented with material from one of the other collections or from an additional source, while for some of the longest parts of the *Compendium* the compilers went outside of Purchas, the Churchills, Campbell, and Barclay to primary sources. The voyages of Columbus (I, 1– 129), for example, were all from the Churchills' collection, but the voyages of Vasco da Gama (I, 130–57) and Pedro Alvares de Cabral (I, 158–77) were extracted, except for one short passage, entirely from a translation made by James Gibbs of Jeronimo Osorio da Fonseca's *De rebus Emmanuelis*

---

[5] *A Compendium of Authentic and Entertaining Voyages, Digested in a Chronological Series* (London, 1766), I, iii.

regis Lusitaniae gentis (Lisbon, 1571), and called in English the *History of the Portuguese, during the Reign of Emmanuel* (2 vols.; London, 1752; I, 36–121). The sole source for the voyages of Cortes (I, 179–286; II, 1–181) was Thomas Townsend's translation of Antonio de Solís y Ribadeneyra's *Historia de la conquista de Mexico* (Madrid, 1684). The compilers used the revision made by Nathaniel Hooke (2 vols.; London, 1738) rather than the original edition of 1724.⁶ "The Discovery and Conquest of Peru by Francis Pizarro" (II, 183–261) combined two versions—one by Campbell, the other by Barclay. Smollett in his narrative of Drake (III, 65–119) supplemented Campbell and Purchas with Nathaniel Crouch's *The English Hero, or Sir Francis Drake Reviv'd* (13th ed.; London, 1739). The reports of Wafer (V, 244–312) and Dampier (VI, 1–122) were taken from the standard text in Knapton's *Collection of Voyages* (4 vols.; London, 1729). Woodes Rogers' *Cruising Voyage round the World* (London, 1726) and Richard Walter's *Voyage round the World, of the Right Honourable George Lord Anson* (London, 1748) were the main sources for the last two sections. The more the subject is pursued, the more is revealed the wide range of the sources and the critical acumen of the editor and his assistants. It should not be overlooked that Purchas, the Churchills, Campbell, and Knapton were in their day conscientious editors who prepared texts that were accepted as both standard and often primary by the eighteenth century. For the majority of the sections, therefore, the *Compendium* was extracted from the fullest and the most original sources, and only fourteen of the twenty-seven articles were limited to one source. All in all, forty-six separate sources were drawn upon. Certainly, Smollett carried out the letter and the spirit of his contract and prepared *A Compendium of Authentic . . . . Voyages*—authentic because they were "from the best books on these subjects extant."⁷

⁶ Dr. Martz has called my attention to the fact that Smollett used the 1738 edition rather than the 1724 edition.

⁷ For a fuller discussion of the sources of the *Compendium* see Martz, *The Later Career of Tobias Smollett*, pp. 30–42, and Appendix I. I am indebted for a number of details to the above book by Dr. Martz, who carried the study of the sources further than I was able to a number of years ago.

The second part of the title promises *Entertaining Voyages*. In the Preface, Smollett was very explicit on what was done to make the voyages entertaining:

So many collections of Voyages have been already given to the world, that the compiler of the ensuing volumes thinks it incumbent upon him to explain the motives which have induced him to swell the number of these productions. One of his principal views in undertaking the work, was to disincumber this useful species of history from a great deal of unnecessary lumber, that tended only to clog the narration and burthen the memory.

We live in an age of levity and caprice, that can relish little besides works of fancy; nor do we listen to instruction unless it be conveyed to us under the pleasing form of entertainment. But to mix profit with delight should be the aim of all writers, and the business of every book: and nothing can contribute more to these valuable ends, than a detail of Voyages; in which we can travel to the most distant corners of the world without stirring from our closets, choose the most entertaining route, embark with the most agreeable companions, view remote cities and their governments, extend our acquaintance thro' all the nations of the globe, and interest ourselves in a succession of incidents and adventures, that at once improve the mind and delight the imagination.

These purposes, we apprehend, have not been fully answered by the voluminous collections which have hitherto appeared in this country: the size and price of a folio are sufficient to intimidate an ordinary reader from purchasing the work or perusing its contents. Besides, they are generally so stuffed with dry descriptions of bearings and distances, tides and currents, variations of the compass, leeway, wind and weather, sounding, anchoring, and other terms of navigation, that none but meer pilots, or sea-faring people, can read them without disgust.

Our aim has been to clear away this kind of rubbish in such a manner as to leave the narrative less embarrassed, but more succinct: we have not only retrenched the superfluities, but endeavoured to polish the stile, strengthen the connexion of incidents, and animate the narration, wherever it seemed to languish.[8]

Whether or not Smollett had Swift in mind when he formulated his editorial criteria, a comparison of the style of the *Compendium* with that of *Gulliver's Travels* supplies a clue to the basic deficiency in the *Compendium*. Years previously Swift had in *Gulliver's Travels* professed much the same procedure as Smollett's:

This Volume would have been at least twice as large, if I had not been bold to strike out innumerable Passages relating to the Winds and Tides, as well as to the Variations and Bearings in the several Voyages; together with the minute Descriptions of the Management of the Ship in Storms, in the Style of Sailors: Likewise the Account of Longitudes and Latitudes; wherein I have Reason to apprehend that Mr. *Gulliver* may be a little dis-

[8] *Compendium*, I, i–iii.

satisfied: But I was resolved to fit the Work as much as possible to the general Capacity of Readers.[9]

For the average reader, Smollett and his assistants, like Swift, did indeed enhance the pleasure of reading the voyagers by "retrenching the superfluities" of nautical statistics, which were of the greatest value to navigators but of little interest to others. He retained, moreover, almost unchanged except in their order, the many descriptions of natural history, social customs, and the like. He and his assistants competently condensed and synthesized the various adventures into a consistent and uniform narrative—"as it were, The Annals of Navigation." In commending the volumes in the *Critical Review*, especially to "our fair country-women," Smollett dwelt upon what had been gained by the excisions, condensations, rearrangements, and the polishing of the style, observing that

nothing can certainly be pleasanter than to sail round the globe in one's easy chair, to make the discovery or conquest of a new world without the least danger from winds and waves, and amuse ourselves with the description of savage laws and customs without fear of being *scalp'd* or *devour'd* by *Indians* and *Cannibals;* besides, that the instruction arising from them, will, for the most part, afford us a much more rational entertainment than the fashionable study of idle novels and romances, which are perpetually pouring in upon us.[10]

In spite of all the changes carried out in revising the material, the modern reader will almost invariably judge Smollett's sources to be more authentic and entertaining than the *Compendium*. For the twentieth century it is the letter and not the spirit that establishes authenticity. What is more, from Smollett's day to the present, general readers, as well as scholars, have found the style of the voyagers and travelers, which Swift wisely imitated, far more entertaining than the style of the *Compendium*. The eighteenth-century historian, with his balanced construction, his enumerations, and his latinized vocabulary, effaced the originality and charm of the voyager, with his loosely constructed sentences, disordered

[9] *The Prose Works of Jonathan Swift*, ed. Herbert Davis (Oxford, 1941), XI, xxxvii–xxxviii.

[10] *Critical Review*, I (May, 1756), (309–12) 309.

plan, and wonderfully idiomatic and concrete vocabulary.
Even the voyagers sensed the distinction, and Woodes Rogers, the loquacious and hardheaded circumnavigator whose
book is second only to Dampier's in lasting appeal, boasted
in the opening paragraph of his *Cruising Voyage round the
World*, "tho others, who give an Account of their Voyages,
do generally attempt to imitate the Stile and Method which
is us'd by Authors who write ashore, I rather chuse to keep
to the Language of the Sea, which is more genuine and
natural for a Marioner." As a result of Rogers' method, his
account of Alexander Selkirk, for example, is far more entertaining than the retelling in the *Compendium*.[11]

In the last analysis the compilers of the *Compendium*,
through synthesizing the narrative, failed to animate it. The
voyagers themselves, their personalities, comments, anecdotes, and allusions are missing. Half the pleasure in reading
the descriptions of foreign lands comes from the character
of the traveler himself and his reactions; delete these and the
results may be a good eighteenth-century history but a dull
travel book. Swift appreciated this fact, and though he was
"bold to strike out innumerable Passages relating to Winds
and Tides, as well as to the Variations and Bearings in the
several Voyages; together with the minute Descriptions of the
Management of the Ship in Storms, in the Style of the Sailors:
Likewise the Account of Longitudes and Latitudes," he kept
Gulliver in the center of the stage and through him animated
the narrative.

A second editorial commission further increased Smollett's
knowledge of travel literature, this time of the Grand Tour.
On May 26, 1753, a few weeks after Smollett signed the
memorandum for the *Compendium*, he contracted with
George Drummond to prepare for the press the travel letters
of his brother Alexander Drummond. The book was published in 1754 as *Travels through Different Cities of Germany,
Italy, Greece, and Several Parts of Asia, as Far as the Banks of
the Euphrates: In a Series of Letters, by Alexander Drum-*

---

[11] Cf. *Compendium*, VII, 183–85, and *A Cruising Voyage round the World* (London, 1712), pp. 125–31.

mond, Esq., His Majesty's Counsel at Aleppo. The letters appear to be based on genuine epistles sent by Drummond to his brother from July 20, 1744, to November 13, 1750, but the originals, as well as Drummond's other letters, are not extant, and hence it is impossible to do more than conjecture as to the changes and additions made by Smollett. In return for his "executing" and "management," to use his own words, Smollett received a hundred guineas, a fact which implies that his services though vaguely designated were nevertheless extensive.[12] He certainly polished the style, and he may have inserted some of the cross-references and allusions to Addison, Breval, De Tournefort, and other travelers.[13] The letters which deal with Europe are better from every point of view than those on the Near East, a difference which may indicate that Smollett carried out a more thoroughgoing revision of the European material, with which he was familiar.

In addition to the customary sights of the Grand Tour, Drummond took notice of festivals, theatrical productions, religious ceremonies, and social customs. He remarked that, though, as he protested, his days of gallantry were past, he found the Greek and Turkish ladies, in the language of Lady Mary Wortley Montagu, "wantonly superbe."[14] In Syria and Cyprus he busied himself with antiquity, geography, and to a less degree, people. His sturdy provincialism blinded him to any good in either Europeans or Asiatics, and the anachronisms in Italian art filled his good Protestant soul with scorn. Most of his comparisons were with Scotland, which was his home, or with Sweden, where he had once traveled. Were it not that Drummond enlisted the aid of Smollett, it is doubtful if his book would be at all remembered today.

Along with his work on the *Compendium* and Drummond's *Travels*, Smollett prepared a volume of translations from the

[12] *Letters*, pp. 24–25, 29, and 133–34.

[13] Drummond, *Travels* (London, 1754): Addison, pp. 2, 11, 14, 18, 24, 25, 26, 29, 34, 38, 44, 58, 61, 67, 86, 88, 150; Misson, p. 166; Breval, p. 167; De Tournefort, p. 169; and Maundrell, p. 199.

[14] *Ibid.*, pp. 143–44 and 179.

Journal oeconomique with the title *Select Essays on Commerce, Agriculture, Mines, Fisheries, and Other Useful Subjects* (London, 1754), "the translation," according to the Preface, "being undertaken at the desire of several persons of taste and distinction, who thought it might conduce to the improvement of useful knowledge." Among the thirty-five essays are, according to Smollett, "authentic accounts of countries and nations, which are but little known to the generality of man-kind," specifically Russia, Denmark, Vienna, Genoa, France, and Lapland—the subject matter of the essays on Lapland being repeated later in a series of articles in the *British Magazine*. A second volume was promised, "provided this meets with that encouragement which, we hope, it will be found to deserve," a hope apparently disappointed, for no second volume is known.

Of all Smollett's journalistic enterprises, however, the *Critical Review* is biographically and historically the most important, and yet unfortunately it stands as a stumbling block to a fuller understanding of Smollett and his acquaintance with contemporary travel literature. He asserted that as a manager for the first seven years, from 1756 to 1763, he wrote a "Great Part of the Critical Review";[15] but reviews and articles can be assigned to him only on the basis of cross-references, stylistic tests, and an intimate knowledge of his life and habits. There is, indeed, the presumption that, as a result of his own travels and his editorship of the *Compendium* and Drummond's *Travels*, he is the author of many of the reviews of travel books which appeared during his association with the journal. In general, however, periodical reviews are impersonal and hence of secondary biographic value even when the author is known. They are commentaries on an age, chiefly valuable for the literary historian, and it is best to accept the *Critical Review* in the spirit in which it was written as embodying the current standards and tastes of Smollett and his enlightened contributors and readers.

Biographically considered, however, the *Critical Review* does show how Smollett enlarged his knowledge of travel

15 *Letters*, p. 81.

books and what use he made of the knowledge. A typical example is his probable notice of A. F. Büsching's *New System of Geography* (6 vols.; London, 1762),[16] which he later consulted for his *Travels*.[17] In the review of Büsching's work he complained bitterly of hackwork on geographies, praised Büsching's labors on all scores, and went on to commend the study of geography. In the preceding month Smollett's history of Denmark (including Norway) in the *Modern Universal History* had appeared. With the material freshly in mind, he now examined carefully Büsching's account of Norway, noting sources, pointing out slight omissions, questioning etymologies, and, in general, displaying his erudition. He praised Thomas Jeffery's translation of G. F. Müller's *Voyages from Asia to America* as "fraught with good sense, abounding in entertainment, and extremely agreeable, from the simplicity of the narrative, and the candour of the journalist."[18] Later he borrowed for his *Travels* a passage from Müller on Kamchatka.[19]

Smollett could also have his joke. In reviewing J. Wilkinson's *The Seaman's Preservation*,[20] an entirely reasonable proposal for constructing life belts of cork, he turned to the Right Reverend Erich Pontoppidan's *Natural History of Norway* (London, 1755) for an "authentic" instance of mermen with which to recruit the English navy as more able to care for themselves in a disaster than seamen armed with Wilkinson's life belt. Not content with one instance, he went on to propose Pez Nicoloa, the swimmer in Goethe's *Der Taucher*, whose story Smollett had read in Fray Benito Jerónimo Feijóo y Montenegro's *Theatro crítico universal*, a kind of "vulgar errors" compilation gathered from all over the

[16] *Critical Review,* XII, 237–50. This notice is ascribed to Smollett only on the internal evidence summarized above.

[17] *Travels*, p. 147.

[18] *Critical Review*, XIII (May, 1762), 405–11.

[19] *Travels*, p. 36; cf. G. F. Müller, *Voyages from Asia to America* (London, 1764), p. 9.

[20] *Critical Review*, VIII (August, 1759), 154–56. This review is assigned to Smollett on the basis of the style and humor, because it defends reviewing as a profession and displays an extensive knowledge of a seaman's life.

world and extending to many volumes.[21] Without naming his sources, he took still a third merman from Padre Feijóo's story of Francisco de la Vega.[22]

Not all the thirty-odd reviews of travel books that were written by Smollett and his associates during the seven years of his managership are, however, as rewarding as these. Many consist merely of summaries and quotations, corrections of errors, comments on style or utility or originality, with a few rare observations of critical value. The following scattered passages summarize with a degree of eloquence the prevailing attitude of the *Critical Review:*

> Could we see a man set out upon this journey, not with an intent to consider rocks and rivers, but the manners and the mechanic inventions, and the imperfect learning of the inhabitants, resolved to penetrate into countries as yet little known, and eager to pry into all their secrets, with an heart not terrified at trifling dangers, if there could be found a man who could unite thus true courage with sound learning, from such a character we might hope much information. Even though all he should bring home was only the manner of dying red in the Turkish manner, his labours would be more beneficial to society, than if he had collected all the mutilated inscriptions, and idle shells on the coast of the Levant.[23]

The last sentiment was warmly espoused by Edward Clarke three years later in his *Letters concerning the Spanish Nation,* which, with an eye on the Addisonian traveler, he prefaced with the refreshing comment:

> For this hath ever appeared to him to be the true and proper design of *Travelling,* to bring back such notices of foreign countries, as may correct any prejudices and errors we have entertained concerning them; such as may improve our present opinions, and contribute to form a just idea of different nations. This employment may be more useful, though, perhaps not so flattering to the imagination, as that of reading *Virgil* upon the banks of the *Mincio, Horace* upon the *Aufidus,* or *Homer* upon the *Scamander.* Writers of authentic accounts of countries, though beneath the attention of elegant genius, and not rising to the higher claims of taste and *virtú,* may notwithstanding be more serviceable to the public, than the purchaser of a decayed *Titian,* the recoverer of a rusty *coin,* the copier of a defaced *inscription,* or the designer of an old *ruin.*[24]

[21] *Theatro crítico universal* (Madrid, 1760), Vol. VI, Discurso Octavo, Nos. 1–18.

[22] *Ibid.,* Nos. 19 ff.

[23] *Critical Review,* VII (June, 1759), 505.

[24] *Letters concerning the Spanish Nation* (London, 1763), p. i. For review see *Critical Review,* XV (April, 1763), 295–302.

For the travelers the highest praise in the *Critical Review*, however, was reserved for Charlevoix and Lady Mary Wortley Montagu. Save for a Jesuitical bias irritating to Englishmen, Charlevoix was an ideal traveler, and he left one of the great stories of exploration in his monumental *Journal of a Voyage to North America*. The *Critical Review*'s praises were unqualified:

A Writer of genius renders the most barren subjects fertile and agreeable; like an alchemist, he converts every substance into gold. Our present author possesses this happy talent in a very peculiar manner. Lively, judicious, penetrating, and observing; nothing escapes his notice; with him every subject becomes new and entertaining.[25]

On his departure for France in June, 1763, Smollett surrendered the active direction of the *Critical Review*, which in the same month hailed *The Letters of the Right Honourable Lady M[ar]y W[ortle]y M[ontagu]e*[26] with the words of her editor:

"Besides the vivacity and spirit which enlivens every part [of Lady Mary's letters], and that inimitable beauty which spreads through the whole; besides the purity of style, which it may be justly accounted the standard of the English tongue; the reader will find a more true and accurate account of the customs and manners of the several nations, with whom this lady conversed, than he can in any other author."

The review further asserted that they were "never equalled by any letter-writer of any sex, age, or nation." Although there is no proof that Smollett wrote the review, it is evident to one who reads his *Travels* consecutively with Lady Mary's *Letters* that he imitated them in more than one way.

Finally, something remains to be said of the travel books that Smollett consulted in his work on two long compilations that appear to have occupied him off and on from about 1755 until his death. They are the *Modern Part of the Universal History* (44 vols.; London, 1759–66) and the *Present State*

[25] *Critical Review*, X (November, 1760), (341–57) 341. There is no clear proof that Smollett wrote this review, though it is fairly certain that he read the book. See the volume on North America in the *Modern Part of the Universal History*, Smollett's *History of England*, *Critical Review*, IX (January, 1760), 47–58, and *Present State of All Nations*, VIII, 249–76, where Charlevoix is cited or summarized.

[26] *Critical Review*, XV (June, 1763), 426–35. For Lady Mary's appreciation of Smollett see her *Letters and Works* (London, 1837), III, 106, 199.

of All Nations (8 vols.; London, 1768–69). Here again the identification of his contributions is dependent almost entirely on conjectures from internal evidence, often of the most tenuous kind.[27] About all that can be ventured is this: first of all, Smollett's work on both compilations enormously increased his knowledge of the politics, sociology, and economics of foreign countries, and, second, his knowledge of the more recently discovered countries was ultimately derived almost exclusively from travel books. For example, if, as Martz believes, Smollett read and possibly corrected some part, if not all, of the account of southern and western Africa in the *Modern Part of the Universal History*, then he must have read at second hand such travelers as Linschöten, Pigafetta, Dapper, Barbot, Atkins, Des Marchais, Tafiletta, Bosman, Kolben, and Cavazzi, the latter as translated by Labat—all well-known African travelers generally accessible in the standard English collections of such editors as Astley or in the French collection of Prévost. If he compiled the history of South America, then he read Antonio de Ulloa and worked through the books of Herrera, Garcilaso de la Vega, and Antonio de Solís, all greatly indebted to earlier travelers. It will be remembered that Smollett earlier used Antonio de Solís as a source for the *Compendium*.

What is true of the *Modern Part of the Universal History* is even more true of the *Present State of All Nations*, which, unlike the *Compendium* and the *Modern Part of the Universal History*, bore Smollett's name on the title-page. In preparing this survey, he was even more dependent than in the *Modern Part of the Universal History* on books and reports of travelers, which, in general, he used only in secondary sources. He started off in the first volume[28] by citing at the end of each article a list of sources, usually the works of the well-known geographers—Purchas, the Churchills, Astley, Harris, and a few others—but the substance of the articles for this volume, as well as parts of others, appears to have been drawn from

[27] Martz, "Tobias Smollett and the *Universal History*," *Modern Language Notes*, LVI (January, 1941), 1–14; *The Later Career of Tobias Smollett*, pp. 104–23.

[28] Volume I seems to have survived mostly in a "second edition."

the *Modern Part of the Universal History*. This last was little more than paraphrased in the accounts of Hindustan (VII, 155–209), Africa (VIII, 55–237), and South America (VIII, 370–467). In the description of Scotland (II, 1–150), however, Smollett consulted the most reliable travelers—Wallace, Martin, Defoe, Gibson, and Burt—but the section on Scotland is hardly a fair example, for Smollett had a personal interest in Scottish travel and was something of an authority in his own right. It is to be regretted that the accounts of Scotland and England (II, 151–478, and III, 1–349) are not more accessible, as they constitute one of the best commentaries on eighteenth-century life, in particular on *Humphry Clinker*. Smollett is especially shrewd and fair in his summary of the English character and contemporary manners, and his comments on Scotland[29] are often as devastating as anything he ever wrote of France or England.

The accounts of other countries are often good reading, especially the account of Persia (VII, 247–312), during the course of which Smollett refers to Tavernier, Le Brun, Hyde, Chardin, Kämpfer, La Martinière, Herbert, Gemelli-Careri, Thévenot, Hamilton, and others. The fact that Smollett in the course of an article alludes to many authorities on a given country does not necessarily mean that he is citing his immediate sources. Both in the *Modern Part of the Universal History* and in the *Present State of All Nations* Smollett distinguishes between books from which he derived his information and books to be consulted by the reader for additional material. Perhaps there was a little ostentation in the practice, but in his references he desired to give not so much his sources as a bibliography on the particular subject, and it will be found that his bibliographies are generally rather exhaustive. The point to be emphasized in the *Present State of All Nations* is, however, that in this compilation Smollett again came in contact with the sweep of world travel and worked over, in the words of the title, the *Geographical, Natural, Commercial, and Political History of All the Countries in the Known World*. Not all this work was done prior

---

[29] E.g., *Modern Part of the Universal History*, II, 35–39.

to the *Travels* and *Humphry Clinker*, but enough was completed to have a great influence on both works.

Smollett's contributions and responsibilities in the *Compendium*, in the *Critical Review*, the *Modern Part of the Universal History*, the *Present State of All Nations*, and lesser journalistic undertakings, laborious and often irritating though they may have been, gave him a broad and diversified knowledge of travel books, a tremendous fund of information drawn from their contents, and a critical perspective of what constituted a first-class book of travels. With such knowledge and experience fresh in mind, he abandoned journalism and set about gathering material and writing one of the very finest books on the Grand Tour.

CHAPTER VIII

TRAVELS THROUGH FRANCE AND ITALY

AFTER twelve years of arduous sedentary toil Smollett permanently and seriously impaired his health and was compelled to give up his home in Chelsea and again become a traveler. Disappointed in his several schemes of finding employment in a warmer climate, he eventually went abroad, depending on his limited resources but undoubtedly intending to pay part of his expenses by writing a book of travels.

Smollett's tour did not begin auspiciously. He departed from England in June, 1763, broken in health, bowed in sorrow at the recent death of an only daughter, "traduced by malice, persecuted by faction, abandoned by patrons"— clearly with wormwood in his soul. He sailed for France already an old hand at traveling and in no humor to minimize the ups and downs of road and inn, the abominable state of transportation, and the inadequacy of accommodations for a man of moderate means. Notwithstanding his unremitting labors, he continued hard pressed for money—a situation enforcing strict economy and involving him in a train of petty irritations, inconveniences, and some hardships. Annoyed by such conditions and depressed in body and spirit, Smollett frequently gave vent to irritation and even rage. Many readers and most critics have been unable to overlook Smollett the invalid and enjoy Smollett the traveler.[1]

[1] The disparagement of Smollett's *Travels* began with Laurence Sterne's well-known advice to "tell it to your physician," which was amplified by George Stillman Hillard (*Six Months in Italy* [Boston, 1853], II, 374–78) and many others.

If Smollett had outgrown the naïve and romantic enthusiasm with which one goes abroad for the first time, he had acquired talents rare in most travelers. The great store of knowledge gained from his many journalistic productions and the preparation of his *History of England*, as well as from his study of medicine, literature, and the classics, was seldom surpassed among his traveling predecessors, except by Burnet, and, on the basis of material presented in chapter vii, it may be added that the soundness of his critical judgment on what constituted the acceptable subjects and the form of a travel book was equaled by the authority of few of his contemporaries.

In addition to his learning and experience, Smollett pos-

More recently Mead (*The Grand Tour in the Eighteenth Century*, p. 112) has written: "Smollett has the querulous and petulant tone of a nervous invalid, who sees everything through jaundiced eyes and makes sweeping assertions based upon an occasional unpleasant experience. In no case is it safe to allow him the final word in *judging* any part of the Continent, though his keen eye and marvelous descriptive faculty enable him to picture individual facts and scenes with great accuracy. One might easily gather from his pages a choice collection of vituperative adjectives, usually in the superlative degree, for he taxes the resources of the language to express his disgust at the treatment he received from scoundrels of every sort. Smollett had, indeed, one long series of quarrels with carriage drivers, innkeepers, and servants in his journey through France and Italy. Some of these squabbles were unquestionably due to annoying exactions and petty knavery, but, as he confesses himself, a small additional outlay would have enabled him to avoid most of them."

With all due respect to Professor Mead's wide reading in the literature on the Grand Tour, as well as his own firsthand knowledge of European travel, I would nevertheless point out one or two inconsistencies in his statement, which represents the general run of criticism passed upon the *Travels*. It is not always easy to separate the inns, roads, food, and service of a journey from the historic sights, scenery, people, and art that are the subjects of a travel experience; some are able to do this better than others. Smollett had a special gift for invective; but one gathers in reading Professor Mead's book that, when Smollett directed all his powers against some petty exaction or annoyance, he was expressing with power and finality what all endured and only feebly and inadequately condemned. Smollett had the conviction that there was, or should be, a pleasure in the very means of travel—in good accommodations, well-built roads, courteous officials, and that one need not travel with the fortitude of a pilgrim bound for some inaccessible shrine. Further—and this is the point I wish to make—because Smollett demanded honesty, cleanliness, and a modicum of decency and rebelled when he failed to find it, there is absolutely no reason why he was not competent to "judge" the Continent, meaning its people, history, commerce, art, and culture. On these subjects he does not display "a choice collection of vituperative adjectives."

And, after all, there are serious reasons for believing that Smollett was not unlike Mrs. Gummidge of *David Copperfield:* "Yes, yes. I feel more than other people do, and I show it more. It's my misfortun'."

sessed a fair knowledge of foreign languages and literature. He read Latin with facility; Greek he knew to a less degree. He was a felicitous translator of Le Sage and Cervantes; though he may not have been able to speak French in 1750, before he left Boulogne in the autumn of 1763 his command of the language enabled him to mix freely with the French people.[2] By the time he sailed for Italy late in 1764 he had learned sufficient Italian to use to advantage two Italian guidebooks in Rome, though he may never have spoken the language with any fluency.[3] He carried abroad Greek, Latin, French, Spanish, and Italian dictionaries, as well as a library of approximately one hundred and fifty volumes, including all his own works, fifty-eight volumes of the *Universal History*, Shakespeare, Congreve, Homer, Sophocles, Virgil, Horace, Juvenal, and Tibullus.[4] He went armed also with Nugent's excellent guide, *The Grand Tour*, in four volumes, which in turn was indebted to Keysler, Temple, Misson, Addison, Pollnitz, Blainville, Montfaucon, Scoto, and Antonini. With all this bibliographical equipment supplementing his knowledge and literary tastes, Smollett was prepared for an eminently valuable tour.

He traveled the well-beaten routes. Having recuperated by resting during the summer of 1763 at Boulogne, he took the road through Montreuil, Amiens, and Abbeville for Paris, where he stopped at the Hôtel de Montmorency in the *faubourg* St.-Germain. He went sight-seeing with his family, recalled his visit in Paris fifteen years before, and damned the French. On the way to Lyons he passed through Fontainebleau, Moret, Maisonneuve, and Sens, but the exorbitant

---

[2] Moore (*Life*, p. 94) is authority for the assertion that Smollett, on his visit to Paris in 1750, "never attained the power of speaking their [French] language with facility, which prevented him from mixing in their society, and deciding, from his own observation, on their national character." In Smollett's own account, as given in the *Travels* of 1763–64, there is no evidence that he was so handicapped. Also, he went abroad fresh from, if not still engaged in, his editorship of a thirty-volume translation of Voltaire, of which he did "a small part of the translation" and "all the notes historical and critical" of the prose—certainly an excellent preparation for an extended visit to France (Eugène Joliat, "Smollett, Editor of Voltaire," *Modern Language Notes*, LIV [June, 1939], 429–36).

[3] *Travels*, p. 250.   [4] Joliat, *Smollett et la France* (Paris, 1935), pp. 249–53.

prices in Lyons made him hasten to Montpellier, where he
arrived on November 5. Here he engaged the services of a
coachman, Joseph by name, and his berlin for Nice. The
warmer climate of the South began to thaw out his blood
and cheer him up; the valley of the Rhone pleased him; and,
when he reached Nîmes, he bought a guidebook and began
sight-seeing in earnest. He dipped into Roman history, described and criticized art, and even fell into one of the travel
vices of his age when he transcribed for the benefit of his
friends at home an inscription on a tomb. Though he wrote
in sincere appreciation of the Roman temple—the Maison
Carrée, which "enchants you with the most exquisite beauties of architecture and sculpture"[5]—he was not inclined to
pass over without comment hotel accommodations such as
those at Cheval Blanc at Montpellier, which he calls "a most
wretched hovel, the habitation of darkness, dirt, and imposi-
tion."[6] His improving health and mounting spirits received
a rude shock from the rains of Montpellier and from the
alarming diagnosis of his ailment by her celebrated "lanthorn
of medicine," Dr. Fizès; but when he had had the final word
in the ensuing quarrel with the doctor, he felt quite cheerful
and found the inhabitants "sociable, gay, and good-tem-
pered." He soon hastened through Tarascon, Orgon, Aix, Le
Luc, Le Muy, Fréjus, Cannes, and Antibes, and by January
15, 1764, was settled in Nice.

Smollett employed his eight months at Nice in a variety
of pursuits. His first care was to rebuild his health. He bathed
in the Mediterranean, exercised on foot and horseback, observed closely the effect of the climate upon his constitution,
and paid particular regard to his diet. In his leisure he directed his restless mind to a study of the geography and history of the Riviera, studied Italian, and made short excursions to the Roman ruins in the immediate vicinity; nor did
he overlook scenes of contemporary life, mixing in the society
of Nice and conversing freely with the natives. The results
were twofold: his strength returned to a remarkable degree,
and from his observations and studies he drew material for

[5] *Travels*, p. 89.   [6] *Ibid.*, p. 91.

one of the best accounts of Nice that has yet been written.[7]

Smollett continued his Grand Tour into Italy, partly on the advice of his friends in London, partly because he had recovered much of his health, but largely because he "had a most eager curiosity to see the antiquities of Florence and Rome."

> I longed impatiently to view those wonderful edifices, statues, and pictures, which I had so often admired in prints and descriptions. I felt an enthusiastic ardor to tread that very classical ground which had been the scene of so many great atchievements; and I could not bear the thought of returning to England from the very skirts of Italy, without having penetrated to the capital of that renowned country.[8]

Around September 1, 1764, he began the journey in a gondola with four oarsmen and a pilot, sailing along the coast past Monaco, Menton, Ventimiglia, to San Remo the first day, to Noli the second, and on to Genoa late the third day. Smollett enjoyed the sea and the coast towns, but not the innkeepers and their *auberges*, which were a miserable lot. He was pleased with Genoa because he was conversant with her recent history and also because the Genoese nobility had a weakness for extravagant marble palaces which he regarded as commendable.

A few days after arriving in Genoa, he and his party were en route again, sailing the first day to Sestri Levante and the second on to Lerici, from which, "heartily tired of the water," they set out for Pisa. Smollett was surprised and delighted with Pisa—the city, the cathedral, and campanile. He seems to have been unprepared for all the historic splendor of the city; later, when he revised the *Travels* for a second edition, it was the passage on Pisa to which he added the most notes, and in afteryears the pleasure of his first impressions of Pisa remained with him, calling him back to her neighborhood for his closing days.

In Florence, Smollett reveled in the art and history of the ancients and observed with interest and appreciation the treasures of the Renaissance. Satisfied with "having seen all the curiosities of Florence," in October he hired a good travel-

---

[7] For Thomas Seccombe's high praise see *ibid.*, p. xxii.   [8] *Ibid.*, p. 202.

ing coach and set out for Rome through Siena, Radicofani, and Viterbo, observing along the way the many objects of interest pointed out by his guidebook. Comfortably settled in Rome and with his social obligations fulfilled, he bought two Italian guidebooks (one three volumes long), hired "a sober, intelligent fellow" as an attendant, and plunged headlong into a tour of Rome. Nothing is to be gained in tracing his footsteps as he inspected the celebrated monuments ancient and modern; only a reading of his letters can convey the breadth of his interests and the indefatigable industry of his sight-seeing.

The return route to Florence, which he selected on poor advice, involved him in troubles with rascally drivers, lazy innkeepers, and miserable roads before he walked into the city late one night through rain and mud, "fully persuaded that the hardships and violent exercise [he] underwent.... had greatly contributed to the re-establishment of [his] health."[9] Before the threat of approaching winter, he hastened to Nice over the same route he had followed into Italy. His concluding remarks are here quoted in full, as they summarize the beneficial results of the Italian tour:

Thus have I given you a circumstantial detail of my Italian expedition, during which I was exposed to a great number of hardships, which I thought my weakened constitution could not have bore; as well as to violent fits of passion, chequered, however, with transports of a more agreeable nature; insomuch that I may say I was for two months continually agitated either in mind or body, and very often in both at the same time. As my disorder at first arose from a sedentary life, producing a relaxation of the fibres, which naturally brought on a listlessness, indolence, and dejection of the spirits, I am convinced that this hard exercise of mind and body, co-operated with the change of air and objects, to brace up the relaxed constitution, and promote a more vigorous circulation of the juices, which had long languished even almost to stagnation. For some years, I had been subject to colds as a delicate woman new delivered. If I ventured to go abroad when there was the least moisture either in the air, or upon the ground, I was sure to be laid up a fortnight with a cough and asthma. But, in this journey, I suffered cold and rain, and stood, and walked in the wet, heated myself with exercise, and sweated violently, without feeling the least disorder; but, on the contrary, felt myself growing stronger every day in the midst of these excesses.[10]

9 *Ibid.*, p. 301.   10 *Ibid.*, pp. 307–8.

His old rancor forgotten, body and spirit strengthened, Smollett, after a short rest at Nice, headed northward, eager to be back with friends in London. He was in no haste in either the stages or the long narrative of the journey. Departing from Nice on February 15, he passed over the mountains to Turin, on to Antibes, Toulon, Marseille, Aix, Avignon, Orange, Paris, and did not reach Boulogne until the middle of June. A month later he was in London, Brewers Street, Golden Square. With some misgivings Smollett, ten months later, in May, 1766, published in two volumes *Travels through France and Italy, Containing Observations on Character, Customs, Religion, Government, Police, Commerce, Arts and Antiquities, with a Particular Description of the Town, Territory, and Climate of Nice.*

In conformity with the almost universal practice of travelers, Smollett presented observations, no matter whether they were originally set down in a journal or in personal letters, in the form of a series of familiar letters—a form adopted even for encyclopedic surveys by Defoe, the geographic and economic gazeteer; Charlevoix, the royal investigator; and Keysler and Misson, the compilers of guidebooks.

As a result of tradition, fashion, and classical precedent, the familiar letter flourished as the most popular and varied prose form in the eighteenth century. Originating with the late Greek and Latin writers, the letter was naturalized in England during the Renaissance and in succeeding years was widely cultivated by Englishmen ranging from Breton's and Suckling's "found" letters, Hall's informative letters, Mrs. Katherine Philips' and the Duchess of Newcastle's social letters, and the familiar letters of Howell's *Epistolæ Ho-Elianæ* to the controversial epistles of scholars, the periodical letters of Addison and Steele, and the fictitious letters of Goldsmith's *Citizen of the World.* Swift fought Ireland's battles in the *Drapier Letters,* Shaftesbury philosophized in a *Letter concerning Enthusiasm,* and Young stimulated literary criticism with *Conjectures upon Original Composition,* as did also Hurd with *Letters on Chivalry and Romance.* The eighteenth century cultivated the letter with exempla, handbooks, grammars, stylebooks, elaborating and illustrating the form with all the completeness of the medieval grammarian. Samuel Richardson's *Familiar Letters on Important Occasions* was but one of the many handbooks that were to be found on every bookseller's shelves. Taken along with much other evidence, the eleven model letters for a young lady's trip to London in Richardson's collection only tend to prove that the familiar letter was the acceptable medium for travel experiences.[11]

The most perplexing problem for succeeding generations has been not the diversity in the form of letters but the authenticity of the contents. Fundamentally, a familiar letter is a direct and intimate communication from one person to another and has customarily been accepted at face value, more than almost any other written record, as conveying trustworthy information. Such letters are familiar in the original sense of the word: that is, letters written within the circle of the family and between close friends. On the other hand, when a writer, though he addresses only one recipient, envisages more than one, when the material is selected and presented formally and with conscious artistry, the letter becomes a familiar letter in the sense that, though no longer personal, it is still a friendly, informal communication of information and ideas. Finally, when the recipient, and, at times, the author, is imaginary, the letter is fictitious.

The confusion comes, not in these distinctions, but in the failure of students to realize that personal letters may serve as a source for familiar or fictitious letters and that a writer may re-work personal letters sent home from a tour into familiar letters addressed to a wider public by reducing the personal allusions and intimate details, by combining material of more general interest from several letters, by consciously polishing the style, and by adding literary or historical al-

[11] For further discussion of the letter as a literary form see especially Harold Cook Binkley, "Letter Writing in English Literature" (unpublished dissertation, Harvard University, 1923); Katherine Gee Hornbeak, *The Complete Letter-writer in English* ("Smith College Studies in Modern Language," Vol. XV [Northampton, 1934]); *Familiar Letters on Important Occasions*, ed. Brian W. Downs (London, 1928); and Richmond P. Bond, "Eighteenth Century Correspondence: A Survey," *Studies in Philology*, XXXIII (October, 1936), 572–86.

lusions. This appears to have been the procedure of the first writer of familiar letters of travel, James Howell, in his *Epistolæ Ho-Elianæ* (4 vols.; London, 1645–55), which include many letters on European travel. Howell, confined in Fleet Prison and compelled to write for his bread, almost certainly took his "Letters and Papers," seized in 1642 but later returned, and re-worked them into a series of familiar letters for the press. The letters as they now stand were clearly not sent by Howell to his friends, and, among all the manuscripts of letters that have survived from the seventeenth century, not one of Howell's has been found that corresponds in all respects with his published letters.[12] Howell knew what he was about, even though some of his critics did not. In the prefatory poem "To the Knowing Reader Touching Familiar Letters"[13] he reviews the contribution of letters to politics, history, philosophy, law, literature, friendship, and love. As for travel letters:

> They can the *Tartar* tell, what the *Mogor*,
> Or the Great *Turk* doth on the Asian Shore:
> The *Knez* of them may know what *Prester John*
> Doth with his Camels in the torrid Zone;
> Which made the *Indian Inca* think they were
> Spirits, who in white Sheets the Air did tear [ll. 15–20].

In his first letter he discusses the style of the familiar letter and observes: "Indeed we should write as we speak; and that's a true familiar Letter which expresseth one's Mind, as if he were discoursing with the Party to whom he writes, in succinct and short Terms," but for letters that have "neither Joints of *Art* nor *Arteries* in them" he has only scorn.[14]

For Howell and later travelers the familiar letter as a literary form was peculiarly well suited to the requirements of the travel book. The universal practice of writing personal letters from abroad to friends at home lent the familiar letter an air of naturalness and reality. It allowed the author to gather the scattered observations of his journal into units larger than the daily entry in a diary or log, and, although it

---

[12] *Epistolæ Ho-Elianæ: The Familiar Letters of James Howell*, ed. Joseph Jacobs (London, 1890–92), II, lxxi-lxxxii.

[13] *Ibid.*, I, 13–15.   [14] *Ibid.*, pp. 17–18.

gradually developed into something like a chapter on one subject,[15] the very evanescent nature of the letter permitted the author to include fragmentary and even sketchy material. Often the only unity in an entire travel book was the consistent point of view of the one writing the letters. In addition to the mechanical advantages, the familiar letter permitted an author to avail himself of all the literary graces of a cultivated and dignified literary form and to elevate his travel book to the rank of the belles-lettres. There is no more revealing comment on the conventions of the familiar letters accepted for over a hundred years than Hester Lynch Piozzi's calm rejection of it as a vehicle for her own observations on her travels:

For the book ——— I have not thrown my thoughts into the form of private letters; because a work of which truth is the best recommendation, should not above all others begin with a lie. My old acquaintance rather chose to amuse themselves with conjectures, than to flatter me with tender inquiries during my absence: our correspondence then would not have been any amusement to the Public.[16]

Smollett, wishing to write a book conforming to recognized literary standards, accepted the familiar-letter form as appropriate for his travels, and six months before his book appeared stated clearly to a friend: "The observations I made in the course of my travels through France and Italy I have thrown into a series of Letters, which will make two volumes in Octavo."[17] Not only from this statement but also from internal evidence it is clear that the *Travels through France and Italy* was not made up of genuine personal letters. Smollett sailed from Nice the beginning of September, 1764, to be gone on his tour of Italy until December, yet Letters XVIII–XXII are dated from Nice in September,[18] October, and No-

[15] E.g., Howell's letters on the Inquisition (I, 290–92), Roman Catholics (I, 618–20), and witches (I, 547–51).

[16] *Observations and Reflections Made in the Course of a Journey through France, Italy, and Germany* (London, 1789), I, vi–vii.

[17] *Letters*, p. 96.

[18] In the first edition of the *Travels*, Letter XVIII is dated May 2, 1764. This is obviously a mistake, as Letter XVI bears the same date, and in the opening paragraph of Letter XVIII Smollett refers to an earlier letter in May on Nice. Smollett in his annotations for a new edition corrected the error and dated Letter XVIII, "Nice, September 2, 1764."

vember, 1764, and describe Nice and not Italy. Furthermore, Letter XVII refers to a murder Smollett saw in Florence, but the letter is dated at least three months before he ever landed in Italy; and the last letter on Italy (XXXV) is dated March 20, 1765, nearly four months after his return to France.

None of the letters in the *Travels* has survived apart from the book, and the relation betweeen Smollett's personal letters and the travel letters that form his book makes it clear that the first were not the basis of the second. Smollett wrote Dr. William Hunter from Nice, February 6, 1764; the contents of this letter, with much additional material, is repeated in Letters XI, XII, and XIII, only the first of which is addressed to a doctor, though not to Dr. Hunter, and appropriately enough discusses the state of medicine in France and Smollett's encounter with Dr. Fizès. Elsewhere for a description of his situation at Nice he refers Dr. Hunter to a letter to Dr. Macaulay, but Letter XII, which would seem to contain this material, is addressed "Dear Sir."[19] In fact, in Letter VIII, addressed "To Mr. M——," Smollett says: "I considered all the letters I have hitherto written on the subject of my travels, as written to your society in general, though they have been addressed to one individual of it." The "society" apparently was a fiction, and the personal salutations to Dr. and Mrs. Moore (VII, VIII), Dr. Smellie (XXXVIII), "Dear Madame" (XV), and the four to "Dear Doctor" (XVI, XVIII, XXI, and XL)—only eight in all out of forty-one letters—were included, not as vestiges of original letters, but because these salutations singled out letters whose contents might be of special interest to the recipients, as, for example, Letter VII to Mrs. Moore, which is on French fashions and gallantry. I have found no example of a travel book in letter form published before 1766 that appears in any respect to be a collection of strictly personal letters, and I believe Smollett's *Travels* was not an exception.

To conclude that the familiar letters in travel books were distinct from personal letters does not mean that travelers

---

[19] For additional evidence on the distinction between Smollett's personal and travel letters see Martz, *The Later Career of Tobias Smollett*, pp. 68–71.

did not imitate the personal letter. The editors of the *Critical Review* as well as the reading public demanded in travel books new and firsthand material gathered by an author from personal observations; and no form carried in its every feature so thoroughly the stamp of authenticity as the personal letter. Few things so bedeviled eighteenth-century readers (and modern scholars) as the numerous fictitious memoirs, correspondences, travels, and other forgeries that were palmed off as genuine personal records, with the result that the public became skeptical on the question of genuineness. It was to this skepticism that Defoe and a host of others addressed long prefaces. No more patently familiar letters could be found than Voltaire's *Letters concerning the English Nation;* yet, in the Preface, Lockman, the translator, says:

> We must . . . . confess, that these Letters were not design'd for the Public. They are the Result of the Author's Complacency and Friendship for Mr. *Thiriot,* who had desir'd him, during his Stay in *England,* to favour him with such Remarks as he might make on the Manners and Customs of the *British* Nation. 'Tis well known that in a Correspondence of this kind, the most just and regular Writer does not propose to observe any Method. Mr. *de Voltaire* in all Probability follow'd no other Rule in the Choice of his Subjects than his particular Taste, or perhaps the Queries of his Friend. Be this as it will, 'twas thought that the most natural Order in which they cou'd be plac'd, would be that of their respective Dates. . . . .
> The Reader will no doubt observe, that the Circumstances in every Letter which had not an immediate relation to the Title of it, have been omitted. This was done on purpose; for Letters written with the Confidence and Simplicity of personal Friendship, generally include certain Things which are not proper for the Press. . . . . The Variety of the Subjects, the Graces of the Diction, the Solidity of the Reflexions, the delicate Turn of the Criticism; in fine, the noble Fire, which enlivens all the Compositions of Mr. *de Voltaire,* delight the Reader perpetually.[20]

The imitation of the personal letter by writers of travel books began with a salutation to a friend, though decorum required that initials alone be given, and concluded with a place and date. In the first letter the traveler informs the recipient, and incidentally the reader, that he writes only because of his friends' requests and solicitations.[21] Clarissa

---

[20] *Letters concerning the English Nation* (London, 1733), sig. A$_3^r$–A$_4^r$.

[21] As early as 1700 William King opened a parody on travel books with the words: "My Lord, You command me to give you a Minute account of what I observed"

Harlowe would never have become entangled in her unfortunate correspondence with Lovelace[22] if her Uncle Hervey had not solicited travel letters from his gifted pen. Under the pretense of addressing friends, the traveling author was at liberty to expatiate on personal habits, common ties of interest, individual tastes, and intimate experiences, often by this means weaving into his book a connecting thread of narrative. Some travelers dwelt on the hardships of the journey, others complained of their health, and not a few set themselves up as connoisseurs in art and antiquity. The best of them returned from time to time to a congenial subject; one remembers Addison on ancient coins, Lister on naked statues, Johnson on trees in Scotland, Baretti on Spanish children, Lady Mary on vaccination, Voltaire on the Quakers, and Fielding on good food. With few exceptions the foremost books of travel in the eighteenth century derived their main interest and value from the fact that they were written in the form of familiar letters containing personal allusions. As has been seen, Lockman, in introducing Voltaire's *Letters*, dwelt upon the intimate tone of the observations, and the same point is made in numerous other prefaces, notably those of Charlevoix's *Journal of a Voyage to North America*, *The Ingenious and Diverting Letters* of the Countess d'Aulnoy, *The Letters of the Right Honourable Lady Mary Wortley Montague*, and Fielding's *Journal of a Voyage to Lisbon*.

(*A Journey to England* [London, 1700], p. 1); Drummond (or more probably Smollett) confessed: "Before I left Engand, I well remember how much I was desired and even importuned by many of my Friends, and you in particular, to communicate in a series of letters, any useful or entertaining observations I should have occasion to make in the course of my peregrinations" (*Travels* [London, 1754], p. 1). Johann Georg Keysler opens his encyclopedic guidebook: "Being safely arrived at *Schaffhausen*, a few days ago, I was not unmindful of your commands and my promise, to give you a true and circumstantial account of every particular occurrence in my travels which I should judge worthy of observation" (*Travels through Germany, Bohemia, Hungary, Switzerland, Italy, and Lorrain* [London, 1756], I, 1); Dr. Moore, in a passage too long to quote, indulges in the same excuse for his letters and goes on to limit and defend his subject matter (*A View of Society and Manners in France, Switzerland, and Germany* [London, 1768], I, 11–14). Another excellent earlier example is to be found in the opening pages of Marie-Catherine, Countess d'Aulnoy's *The Ingenious and Diverting Letters of the Lady —— Travels into Spain* (London, 1691).

[22] See *Clarissa*, Letter III.

Smollett did not open his book with a preface asserting the authenticity of his letters, but he adopted all the other conventions of the form. His use of the place and date line, while consistent, did not entirely correspond to his actual itinerary; to a less extent he employed the salutation as a means of conveying a sense of the intimacy of his letters. However, he began his book in the customary fashion:

> DEAR SIR,—You laid your commands upon me at parting, to communicate from time to time the observations I should make in the course of my travels, and it was an injunction I received with pleasure. In gratifying your curiosity, I shall find some amusement to beguile the tedious hours, which, without some such employment, would be rendered insupportable by distemper and disquiet.

Faced with the fact that his subject, aside from what he observed at Nice, lacked both novelty and freshness after several generations of Englishmen had taken the Grand Tour and described it, Smollett sharpened his humorous and satiric pen, polished his style, brought into play his skill in anecdotes and literary references, and indulged in personal allusions. For descriptions of all the usual sights of the Grand Tour he was content to refer his readers to Keysler, of whom he wrote:

> Those who would have a particular detail of every thing worth seeing at Florence, comprehending churches, libraries, palaces, tombs, statues, pictures, fountains, bridges, &c. may consult Keysler, who is so laboriously circumstantial in his descriptions, that I never could peruse them, without suffering the headache, and recollecting the old observation, That the German genius lies more in the back than in the brain[23].

While there was little observed by his predecessors that Smollett failed to notice and record, he wrote best on the subjects that interested him personally. He bore Addison company in his study of classical poets, classic statuary, and Roman life, and now and then found him at fault.[24] All his classical learning he brought to bear on whatever he saw—palaces, ruins, galleries, statues, the Tiber—and, with D'Arnay, he was interested in the private life of the Romans. The subject of

---

[23] *Travels*, p. 239; see also pp. 158 and 284; cf. *Critical Review*, IV (September, 1757), 185.

[24] *Travels*, pp. 235, 244, and 294.

Roman food, already broached in *Peregrine Pickle*, was pursued again with the aid of Apicius, and, riding his hobbyhorse on hygiene, he examined sewage disposal in ancient Rome and found much to be desired. He was shocked at the cruelty of the ancient Romans, pleased with their baths, and scornful of their navy. After a careful examination of classical evidence on the latter subject, Smollett concluded: "I do believe in my conscience that half a dozen English frigates would have been able to defeat both the contending fleets at the famous battle of Actium, which has been so much celebrated in the annals of antiquity, as an event that decided the fate of empire."[25] If he lacked reverence for certain things ancient, his was certainly not an irreverence born of ignorance; if he judged harshly and independently, he was no less honest and actuated by common sense.

He maintained much the same attitude toward both classic and modern art; he kept company with Gray, Webb, and Bianchi in the modern galleries but was guided and moved by his own standards.[26] His reactions often contradicted what tradition, fashion, and the fashionable guidebooks decreed, and his contemporaries never forgave him. Most of the adverse criticism directed against him is forgotten, and it is no longer necessary to take up the cudgel in Smollett's defense. One example of Smollett's judgment on aesthetic matters will bear repetition, since it occasioned the famous encounter between Smollett and Sterne, of which only Sterne's version is usually quoted. Sterne, it will be recalled, met the "learned Smelfungus" on the steps of the Pantheon: " 'Tis nothing but a huge cock-pit,' " said Smelfungus; to which Sterne rejoined, "I wish you had said nothing worse of the Venus of Medicis, for in passing through Florence, I had heard he had fallen foul upon the goddess, and used her worse than a common strumpet, without the least provocation in nature."[27] Here is the passage that supplied Sterne with the occasion for his sneer:

[25] *Ibid.*, p. 274.

[26] *Ibid.*: Webb, p. 282; Bianchi, pp. 235 and 237.

[27] *A Sentimental Journey* (London, 1769), pp. 33–34 ("In the Street, Calais").

With respect to the famous Venus Pontia, commonly called *de Medicis*,
which was found at Tivoli, and is kept in a separate apartment called the
Tribuna, I believe I ought to be intirely silent, or at least conceal my real
sentiments, which will otherwise appear equally absurd and presumptuous.
It must be want of taste that prevents my feeling that enthusiastic admiration with which others are inspired at sight of this statue: a statue
which in reputation equals that of Cupid by Praxiteles, which brought such
a concourse of strangers of old to the little town of Thespiæ. I cannot
help thinking that there is no beauty in the features of Venus; and that the
attitude is aukward and out of character. . . . . Without all doubt, the
limbs and proportions of this statue are elegantly formed, and accurately
designed, according to the nicest rules of symmetry and proportion; and
the back parts especially are executed so happily, as to excite the admira
tion of the most indifferent spectator.[28]

He concludes the description with a parade of learning that
is beside the point for the present purpose. Here is knowledge,
frankness, modesty, and at least a laudable desire to discover
the beauty that he did not discern; and, according to Thomas
Seccombe, it can now be said that "cultivated opinion has
since come round to his side."[29] There is no need to multiply
instances of the same kind; Seccombe has thoroughly examined this vexing question of Smollett's opinions of art and
has decided in his favor.[30] Though in a very amusing tour
through the Palais-Royal in *Peregrine Pickle* he may have
held up to ridicule a foolish ignorant connoisseur, Pallet—if
Pallet can lay claim to that title—Smollett was at all times
respectful of the qualified critic and repeatedly disclaimed
any authority for his own assertions.[31]

After all, I do not set up for a judge in these matters . . . . I am used to
speak my mind freely on all subjects that fall under the cognizance of my
senses; though I must as freely own, there is something more than common sense required to discover and distinguish the more delicate beauties
of painting.[32]

Remembering then that in the many pages of the *Travels* devoted to a survey of the galleries of Florence and Rome the
frank opinions of a man of considerable experience and learning, not the dictates of a virtuoso, are set down, one must rel-

[28] *Travels*, pp. 235–36.

[29] *Ibid.*, p. li.   [31] *Ibid.*, pp. 252, 264, 281, and 290.

[30] *Ibid.*, pp. xlviii–lvi.   [32] *Ibid.*, pp. 240–41.

ish the good taste and originality of almost all that Smollett wrote.[33]

In his *Travels* he showed that he could descend from the fine arts and, as he had done earlier in *Peregrine Pickle*, prepare another banquet, this time in the manner of the French; savor French food with Lister or, like him, look into the present state of medicine in France; and decry with Walpole and the majority of his compatriots the meanness, levity, and immorality of the public and private life of the French. With the best of the travelers he was not above giving the king of France a little sound advice. Smollett's contemporaries in England applauded, and even in these days the *Travels* made him popular in Germany,[34] but the French have never forgiven him. The book was immediately and harshly reviewed in France, and a noticeable falling-off in the popularity of Smollett's novels and *History* among French readers followed. The Francophile Sterne laughed at him, and later M. Babeau called him "un Anglais de mauvaise humeur,"[35] yet the good

[33] In an investigation of four major printed sources consulted by Smollett on his travels, three of which Smollett mentions (*Travels*, pp. 85, 235 and 237, and 250, the last by title), Martz has perhaps pushed his conclusions on a debatable subject a little too far. He asserts that he has dealt "Smollett's reputation as a scholar . . . . a serious blow" (*The Later Career of Tobias Smollett*, p. 74) when he discloses that Smollett extracted material from these sources for some 40 out of 430 pages in the *Travels*. After all, a man who read through 1,800 octavo pages of the *Roma antica* for scarcely 14 pages in his own book had some sense of thoroughness and discrimination, not to mention disinterested curiosity.

As a matter of fact, Smollett's handling of his sources can be interpreted to his credit as a scholar; and, after all, his scholarship involves the authenticity of his sources, his exceptional veracity (*Travels*, p. xxii), and the validity of his "remarks." Upon none of these subjects has Martz much to offer, though he does admit that Smollett verified his literary borrowings by careful observation (*The Later Career of Tobias Smollett*, pp. 75 and 89). It is expecting a little too much of an eighteenth-century traveler that he give full titles and page references for all his sources, but it is debatable if Smollett deliberately sought to conceal his sources, especially as regards Bianchi, who as "Custode della Galleria Medico-Imperiale di Firenze" doubtless did, as Smollett said, "show the gallery" (*Travels*, p. 237; *The Later Career of Tobias Smollett*, p. 81). In what sense does "erudition . . . . really belong to Smollett" or any of his contemporaries (*The Later Career of Tobias Smollett*, p. 85)?

[34] Joliat, *Smollett et la France*, pp. 111–57, and Harold Wade Streeter, *The Eighteenth Century English Novel in French Translation* (New York, 1936), p. 74.

[35] A. Babeau, *Les Voyageurs en France* (Paris, 1885), pp. 212–34. For a Frenchman who found the *Travels* a very useful book see Joliat, "Millin's Use of Smollett's *Travels*," *Revue de littérature comparée*, XVIII (July–September, 1938), 510–14.

citizens of Nice expressed their gratitude for the publicity by naming La Rue Smolet. If Smollett is to be condemned, it is in the company of his generation, and if nationalism can be defended, then Smollett's *Travels* has its justification. Smollett had much in common with Swift but never more than when he wrote in defense of his characterization of the French:

> When I talk of the French nation, I must again except a great number of individuals, from the general censure. Though I have a hearty contempt for the ignorance, folly, and presumption which characterise the generality, I cannot but respect the talents of many great men, who have eminently distinguished themselves in every art and science: these I shall always revere and esteem as creatures of a superior species, produced, for the wise purposes of providence, among the refuse of mankind.[36]

Drop but the word "French" from this passage and "English" and "French" from many others, and the result is a misanthropy, not unlike Swift's, which still wakens a responsive chord in many thoughtful persons. Smollett was a traveler, not a philosopher, and the contrasts between nations and customs were his bill of fare.

Indifference and perhaps a little toleration have weakened the effect of Smollett's many observations on religion, a subject of perennial interest to English travelers from Bishop Burnet on; some of Smollett's comments are good, especially his famous comparison between Calvinism and tragedy and between Catholicism and comedy. He did not write for Catholic readers, but they should be able to enjoy the following anecdote:

> A poor gentleman of Nice, who piques himself much on the noble blood that runs in his veins, though he has not a pair of whole breeches to wear, complained to me, that his great-grandmother had founded a perpetual mass for the repose of her own soul, at the rate of fifteen sols (ninepence English) a day; which indeed was all that now remained of the family estate. He said, what made the hardship the greater on him, she had been dead above fifty years, and in all probability her soul had got out of purgatory long ago; therefore the continuance of the mass was an unnecessary expence. I told him, I thought in such a case, the defunct should appear before the civil magistrate, and make affidavit of her being at peace, for the advantage of the family. He mused a little, and shrugging up his shoulders, replied, that where the interest of the church was at stake, he did not believe a spirit's declaration would be held legal evidence.[37]

---

[36] *Travels*, p. 60.   [37] *Ibid.*, pp. 171–72.

Besides an enthusiasm for classical antiquity, the fine arts, religion, national differences, and good food, Smollett shared many other interests with his traveling contemporaries. Although he did not travel to Rome to measure the Roman foot as did La Condamine,[38] he had all of that Frenchman's curiosity in science, and he kept a thermometrical table as carefully as Drummond did during his residence in Aleppo. In an appreciation of natural beauty Smollett anticipated succeeding travelers and often turned from antiquity and from men to describe a scene that would have delighted Gray or Pennant or Ruskin.[39] He took particular notice of Salvator Rosa and relished the landscapes, waterfalls, and ruins Rosa selected for his subjects.[40] He studied agriculture with the astuteness of a Young and anticipated Wordsworth when he stopped his carriage to pick some wild crocuses and again later in Nice when he wrote: "When I stand upon the rampart, and look round me, I can scarce help thinking myself inchanted . . . . [and find] plats of roses, carnations, ranunculas, anemonies, and daffodils, blowing in full glory, with such beauty, vigour, and perfume, as no flower in England ever exhibited."[41] Finally, Smollett, more than any other traveler, helped introduce the Riviera to Englishmen. He thereby realized his modest hope that his "Performance may be usefull to other valetudinarians who travel for the Recovery of their Health."[42]

The mass of history, sociology, art criticism, archeology, and natural history comprising the factual substance of the *Travels* would be heavy reading were it not animated by Smollett's own personality. In his *Travels* and later in *Humphry Clinker* Smollett found in the familiar letter a literary form in which he had full liberty to indulge all his propensities for autobiography, and he was under no compulsion to

[38] Charles Marie de la Condamine, *An Extract from the Observations Made in a Tour to Italy* (London, 1768). The tour was made in 1754–56.

[39] *Travels*, pp. 18, 69, 78, 125, 226, and 243.

[40] For a typical comment on Rosa see *ibid.*, pp. 289–90.

[41] *Ibid.*, p. 120.

[42] *Letters*, p. 96.

restrain his predisposition to discuss his contemporaries. He
frankly addressed his friends and discoursed on mutual ties of
taste, association, or interests, both professional and social.
Even more frequently he recounted his experiences on the sea
and on the road with companions, servants, custom officials,
and rapacious publicans, whom he castigated more thoroughly than Fielding did Mrs. Humphreys in the *Journal of a
Voyage to Lisbon* (1755) or Thicknesse did the exorbitant
innkeeper whose bill he had published in a London paper.
Not all readers may relish the reports on his fluctuating
health or believe that his encounter with Dr. Fizès, "the
great lanthorn of medicine," is entirely to Smollett's credit.
He rode his "hygienic horse" with a vengeance as regards
both personal and national habits and was forever adding
new observations and proof to his espousal of the "efficacy of
sea-bathing."[43]

In all such autobiographic passages Smollett is no longer a
detached observer. He participates in the action, and—
without wishing to push the comparison too far—just as
there is something of Smollett in Roderick and Peregrine and
Sir Launcelot Greaves, so there is something of the picaro in
Smollett—a picaro, to be sure, who often loses his sense of
humor but who, in making his way by his own wits, often
unmasks the affectation and baseness of mankind. There are
many episodes in the *Travels* that would not be out of place
in *Peregrine Pickle*, and many passages akin in subject and
spirit to parts of *The Metamorphoses*, *Don Quixote*, *Gil Blas*,
or the *Roman comique*.

Less extensive than the factual part, the passages in which
Smollett expands his personality and enlarges on his adventures are the ones, nevertheless, that animate the narrative
and afford as much pleasure as anything else in the book.
Two examples should suffice to give the personal flavor of the
book, both chosen because they foreshadow two characters in
Humphry Clinker. The first is of Joseph the muleteer who is
the forerunner of the ostler servant Humphry. Joseph in the
Travels is always welcome in the narrative and helps the

43 *Travels*, pp. 7, 13–14, 18, 31, 67, and 191–92.

Rowlandson

Direful consequences of Clinker's aukwardness

reader, as he did Smollett, to while away the long journey southward from Paris. The following scene occurred while the party was passing through the Provence:

One day perceiving a meadow on the side of the road, full of a flower which I took to be the crocus, I desired my servant to alight and pull some of them. He delivered the musquetoon [which Smollett carried to defend himself against robbers] to Joseph, who began to tamper with it, and off it went with a prodigious report, augmented by an eccho from the mountains that skirted the road. The mules were so frightened, that they went off at the gallop; and Joseph, for some minutes, could neither manage the reins, nor open his mouth. At length he recollected himself, and the cattle were stopt, by the assistance of the servant, to whom he delivered the musquetoon, with a significant shake of the head. Then alighting from the box, he examined the heads of his three mules, and kissed each of them in his turn. Finding they had received no damage, he came up to the coach, with a pale visage and staring eyes, and said it was God's mercy he had not killed his beasts. I answered, that it was a greater mercy he had not killed his passengers; for the muzzle of the piece might have been directed our way as well as any other, and in that case Joseph might have been hanged for murder. "I had as good be hanged (said he) for murder, as be ruined by the loss of my cattle,"—

a reflection that prompts Joseph to tell of his own dark past and of his intimacy with the famous bandit Mandrin.[44]

The second example anticipates Smollett's fuller interpretation of himself later in the character of Matthew Bramble. The scene in the *Travels* is again in the Provence. After repeated delays at several posts, at each of which Smollett saw the same person whom he took to be a postmaster directly responsible for the delays, Smollett upbraided the man, only to discover that

he was a man of fashion (un seigneur) who lived in the neighbourhood of Auxerre. I was much mortified to find that I had treated a nobleman so scurvily, and scolded my own people for not having more penetration than myself. I dare say he did not fail to descant upon the brutal behaviour of the Englishman; and that my mistake served with him to confirm the national reproach of bluntness, and ill breeding, under which we lie in this country. The truth is, I was that day more than usually peevish, from the bad weather, as well as from the dread of a fit of the asthma, with which I was threatened: and I dare say my appearance seemed as uncouth to him, as his travelling dress appeared to me. I had a grey mourning frock under a wide great coat, a bob wig without powder, a very large laced hat, and a meagre, wrinkled, discontented countenance.[45]

44 *Ibid.*, pp. 80–81.   45 *Ibid.*, p. 74.

There is one last aspect of eighteenth-century travel books
and in particular Smollett's *Travels* which should be recognized as fundamental in its appeal. The average traveler is
normally interested in contrasts both implied and stated; he
does not study geography, topography, agriculture, society
in city, town, and country for themselves alone but for the
variations and contrasts which arise in comparison with another country. He makes observations on all subjects—
geography, history, government, economics, society, and
science—and in each instance he makes no pretense to completeness, though he may strive to be accurate and unbiased.
But essentially he is writing for people at home, and he en-
deavors to describe the sights which contrast with or illumi-
nate his own native surroundings and culture. For this reason it may be laid down almost as a prerequisite that a traveler must be thoroughly imbued with the history, culture,
current thought, and tastes of his own class, country, or nation; for as the sharpness, variety, and degree of the contrasts
between him and his new surroundings increase, to that extent the value and appeal of his book as a literary record of
travel are enhanced. Fielding asserted that it was in these
contrasts that a man best "acquired knowledge of men and
things." In more recent times Thomas Edward Lawrence,
in his introduction to Doughty's *Travels in Arabia Deserta*,
has, from the point of view of the professional traveler, emphasized the value of national contrasts in these words:

> We export two chief kinds of Englishmen, who in foreign parts divide
> themselves into two opposed classes. . . . . [One class loses its nationality
> and goes native.] The other class of Englishmen is the larger class. In the
> same circumstance of exile they reinforce their character by memories of
> the life they have left. In reaction against their foreign surroundings they
> take refuge in the England that was theirs. They assert their aloofness,
> their immunity, the more vividly for their loneliness and weakness. They
> impress the peoples among whom they live by reaction, by giving them an
> ensample of the complete Englishman, the foreigner intact.
>
> Doughty is a great member of the second, the cleaner class. He says
> that he was never Oriental, though the sun made him an Arab; and much
> of his value lies in the distinction. His seeing is altogether English.[46]

[46] Charles M. Doughty, *Travels in Arabia Deserta* (New York, 1923), I, xviii.

Lawrence's discriminating appraisal of Doughty can be applied with equal significance to many travelers. Addison, the English classicist amid the ruins of ancient Rome; Lady Mary Wortley Montagu, the English lady in the courts of Vienna and Constantinople; Johnson, the Londoner in the Scottish Highlands; Bruce, the Scottish lord in the court of Abyssinia; Kinglake, of Eton and Oxford, in the Near East; and Smollett, the insular Briton traveling through the scenes of contemporary French and Italian life—all these are absorbingly interesting figures because of the contrast in which they stand to their surroundings. It must be emphasized that, although Muralt was able to observe two nations dispassionately, and although most travelers are conscious of the culture of their class or nation and are capable of some objectivity in their evaluations, the more universal and striking contrasts arise when a traveler, in expressing his individual reactions, also speaks unconsciously for the larger social group. In a social survey, a historical examination, or a scientific investigation, strong or marked personal allusions must naturally be eschewed, but in familiar letters they are a part of the fundamental appeal and even value of the best of all travel books. This is why the most interesting travelers from Coryate to Keyserling are often men strongly marked by class or national characteristics.

One need only dip into the *Travels* to become aware of the dominating power of Smollett's personality, his outspoken expression of his own character, and his insularity; but, unlike many other travelers, he intensified, both consciously and unconsciously, the sharpness of the contrasts. His experiences as a journalist and a controversialist had given to his style a richness and incisiveness that in turn tended to give an appearance of exaggeration to all he said. Thus when he censured the French, it was not in general terms, rounded out with colorless phrases, but with a freshness in detail, an idiomatic style, and a concrete vocabulary that make one remember his sharp engravings long after the equally unfair but colorless sketches of his contemporaries are forgotten.

Arnold Bennett, himself a versatile journalist and novelist, grasped on first acquaintance the essential excellence of Smollett as a traveler and set down in his journal what is perhaps the fairest praise ever accorded the *Travels:*

A fine *splenetic* book, thoroughly interesting. The kind of book that a few men might, and probably do, cherish as a masterpiece too special in its flavour to please the crowd. It gives the impression of a sound, sincere personality, not very cultured in the arts, but immensely well informed, and breathing a hard, comfortable common sense at every pore. A doctor's personality, and yet still more the personality of a police magistrate; slightly less *doux*, and more downright, than that of Fielding. One leaves this book in thankfulness that one is not an eighteenth-century traveller.[47]

[47] *The Journals of Arnold Bennett*, ed. Newman Flower (London, 1932), I, 257.

CHAPTER IX

HUMPHRY CLINKER, THE STORY OF
THE LAST JOURNEY

AFTER his return to London in the summer of 1765, Smollett never regained the energy for an active life; remarkable as was his "resuscitation," he was aware that his health was precarious and his years few. All his thoughts and pleasures now turned upon his family and friends, and, although he was frequently subject to the vexations and pains of a semi-invalid, he surveyed life with an increasing cheerfulness and expanded his soul with a warmth and benignity never before apparent. During the summer and autumn of 1765 he busied himself preparing the manuscript of his *Travels* for the press. According to *Pope's Bath Chronicle,* the best-established and most reputable Bath newspaper, he arrived in Bath on October 17, and, benefiting from the waters, he soon took up his residence on the South Parade to settle into the life of a valetudinarian.[1] His thoughts and his heart, however, were in Scotland. As early as November he was longing to be there; and in April,[2] when his constitution took a turn for the worse and the climate and waters of Bath no longer sustained his health, feeling death near, he resolved to return to Scotland.

Fortunately for English letters, his rugged constitution held in reserve strength for six more years of life, and his

[1] For this date and unpublished information on the period of the composition of *Humphry Clinker* and Smollett's final years in Italy, I am indebted to Professor Knapp, "A Study of the Final Period of Tobias Smollett: *The Expedition of Humphry Clinker* and Contributions to the Biography of Tobias Smollett and Ann Smollett" (unpublished dissertation, Yale University, 1928), chaps. i and ii.

[2] *Letters,* pp. 97 and 100.

literary powers were once more stimulated by the toil and
pleasure of travel. In *Roderick Random* he had told of ventur-
ing forth into the world, and again, twenty-six years later,
in the same manner he chronicled in *Humphry Clinker* with
even more autobiographic frankness the last journey home to
Scotland. The stages are more carefully marked, the references to friends and acquaintances less guarded, the clear
personal note more frequent, and the experiences recounted
not so often under the guise of fiction as in the tone of a
trustworthy record. With all the parade and array of dates,
stages, topography, and only thinly veiled description of
personal experience and contemporary events, *Humphry
Clinker* remains, nevertheless, almost as unsatisfactory a
source for biography as *Roderick Random*. Into it were
gathered not only the events of the final journey but also
reminiscences of earlier travels in England and Scotland; and
from this combination it is well-nigh impossible to trace with
any certainty the itinerary, to settle upon dates, or to identify specific events.[3]

According to both the novel and the author's letters, Smollett began his tour about April 1, 1766; he was in Glasgow
with Dr. Moore in August, and he was back in Bath by
November.[4] Probably Smollett went up to London first and
thence took the road north through Harrogate, York, Scarborough, Durham, and Newcastle to Edinburgh. The tour
was continued through the Lowlands to Glasgow and eventually to Cameron, the family seat, from which he made several excursions, for the first time in his life visiting the Highlands and the islands of Islay, Jura,[5] Mull, and Icolmkill. The
return journey carried him south by Lanark, Dumfries, Sol-
way Firth, through Carlisle and back to Bath.

While it would be comforting to assume that Smollett enjoyed the tour with as much enthusiasm and good spirits as
Matthew Bramble, the fact is that he was in miserable health

---

[3] See Chambers, *Smollett*, pp. 130 ff., and Austin Dobson, "The Topography
of 'Humphry Clinker,'" *Eighteenth Century Vignettes* (2d ser.; London, 1894),
pp. 131–60.

[4] *Letters*, pp. 99–100.   [5] Chambers, *Smollett*, pp. 157–58 n.

during much of the journey and returned to Bath afflicted with an ulcerous growth on his forearm.[6] Bramble looked forward to taking the "heath in all weathers," fortified with a "considerable stock of health," but Smollett, every night when he went to bed, "fervently wished that [he] might be dead before morning," so great were his pains and afflictions.[7] As a result of the Scottish tour he recovered enough, however, to make a final bid for a consulship at Nice or Leghorn, this time through his close friend and great Scottish contemporary David Hume, at that time undersecretary of state; but on July 18, 1767, Hume reported that he had consulted Lord Shelburne to no advantage.[8] Shortly afterward, with all bitterness of soul forgotten, he took an affectionate farewell of England and departed "into perpetual exile."

He set out for Italy late in 1768, going first to Lucca, next to the Casa Lenzi on the Ponte Grande, Pisa,[9] in 1769. In the spring of 1770 he moved to a villa two miles out of Leghorn, near Antignano under the shadow of Monte Nero,[10] where he remained until his death on September 17, 1771.

During the course of his last six unsettled years in London and Bath, and his travels in England, Scotland, and eventually Italy, Smollett wrote *Humphry Clinker*, which was published June 18, 1771. He began it during the winter of 1765–66 while in Bath, or perhaps London, and with few later changes carried the story through the Scottish tour before he departed from England for Italy, where only the concluding portion was written.[11] In writing his last novel, Smollett was again stimulated, as in most of his best writings, by his enjoyment of traveling. The tour in *Humphry Clinker* must have

---

[6] *Letters*, pp. 99–102, and Moore, *Life*, I, 133–34.

[7] *Letters*, p. 99.

[8] *Letters of David Hume*, ed. J. Y. T. Greig (Oxford, 1932), II, 151–52.

[9] Chambers, *Smollett*, p. 173; Anderson, *Life of Smollett*, pp. 130–33 (letters from Dr. Armstrong); and John Doran, *'Mann' and Manners at the Court of Florence* (London, 1876), II, 217–18.

[10] *Letters*, pp. 106 and 109–10. See also John Armstrong, *A Short Ramble through Some Parts of Italy and France, by Launcelot Temple* (London, 1771), p. 51.

[11] Knapp, "Study of the Final Period of Tobias Smollett," chap. iii.

given him the greatest pleasure of all: the homeward and
final journey to his friends and country—to Scotland.

At the outset he chose as his model the familiar letter, the
prevailing form for travel books. This choice is confirmed in
one of the prefatory letters in which he has the fictitious
publisher, Mr. Davis, wisely observe: "The taste of the town
is so changeable. Then there have been so many letters upon
travels lately published—What between Smollett's, Sharp's,
Derrick's, Thicknese's, Baltimore's, and Baretti's, together
with Shandy's Sentimental Travels, the public seems to be
cloyed with that kind of entertainment."[12]

Of the seven collections of "letters upon travels" referred
to by Smollett's imaginary Mr. Davis, all but two were cast
in the familiar-letter form. Baltimore's *Tour to the East*
(1767) was composed of the journals he kept on his travels,
and Sterne's impressionistic form is well known. On the other
hand, Dr. Samuel Sharp's *Letters from Italy* (1766) were
modeled on those of his friend Voltaire, each being a short
essay on a separate topic. Philip Thicknesse, in his *Useful
Hints to Those Who Make the Tour of France* (1768), frankly
accepted the familiar letter as a convenient literary fiction.
Samuel Derrick, in the "Advertisement" to his *Letters Written from Leverpoole* (1767), insisted that the collection was
published solely in response to the solicitations of his friends
and that "the letters are now printed as they were originally
written." This last statement can only mean that Derrick
wrote the letters originally for publication. Like all other
familiar letters appearing in travel books, not a single one of
Derrick's *Letters* has survived in any form outside the book.[13]
In the *Journey from London to Genoa* (1770), Baretti also
cast the daily entries of his journal into the form of letters.[14]

So much for the form of books competing with *Humphry
Clinker* for popular favor. Having assigned his novel a place

[12] *Humphry Clinker*, I, 3.

[13] In a private letter of October 10, 1940, Dr. David Little of Harvard University
confirms a statement made several years ago in the course of a conversation, that,
after a long and diligent search, he has "never found the slightest trace of [the]
manuscripts" of Derrick's letters on Ireland.

[14] Before the end of Vol. IV, the letter form is dropped.

among a group of travel books, all published during the years in which he was writing *Humphry Clinker*, Smollett forthwith adopted the familiar letter, the literary form appropriate to the genre, which he had employed in the *Travels* and for which he had immediate models in Sharp, Derrick, Thicknesse, and Baretti. Except for the few concluding letters, in which he concentrates on bringing the plot to a close, Smollett preserved carefully the convention of place and date. He did not, however, arrange the letters in a strict chronological order but more often by subject. There is a general agreement between the dates and places with what is known of Smollett's final tour to Scotland, and this agreement implies that in this respect at least *Humphry Clinker* is founded on a diary or journal.

In addition to giving long and original descriptions of the various countries they visited, the several travelers named by Smollett all expressed personal opinions and recounted personal experiences. It has already been indicated how Smollett personally dominated his *Travels;* Sharp followed Smollett's lead and put himself to the fore, yet he protests in the Preface that the "LETTERS, though now a little altered and curtailed, were not originally intended for the Press." Yorick made his apologies for "a quiet journey of the heart in pursuit of NATURE," by an appeal to the "Great SENSORIUM of the world!"

Thicknesse's personal remarks in his *Useful Hints* were so often made at Smollett's expense that it is a wonder that Smollett included him in the company of popular travelers. Halfway through the composition of his short and chatty *Observations on the Customs and Manners of the French Nation* (1766), Thicknesse received from London a copy of Smollett's *Travels* which pleased him, and thereafter to the end of his book he often alluded to Smollett, in almost every instance to commend or supplement his remarks. The *Critical Review*, however, was so inconsiderate as to speak harshly of Thicknesse's *Observations*, an affront which was sufficient to dispatch the incensed author on a tour for revenge. On the first page of his next book, *Useful Hints to Those Who Make the Tour of France* (1768), he wrote: "I have *accompanied* Mr. Smollet a second time, through his *travels* into France and Italy, and I dare say you will now think me justly intitled to *review* his travels, or rather his *tales*, without laying any other restraint upon my pen, than what *prudence, and attention to myself* dictates." To be sure, Thicknesse did not devote the whole volume to a castigation of Smollett, but he did assail him as often as the opportunity arose and employed the familiar letter to its full capacity as an outlet for all his personal grievances.

In defense of the intimate details in his *Tour to the East* Lord Baltimore said simply, "I wrote . . . . [my journals] for my own private amusement, without any thoughts of their publication."[15] Derrick and Baretti, on the other hand, were more apprehensive because of the intimate tone of their letters, and, as a result, each prefaced his book with a rather significant apology. Derrick wrote:

For many books, that have been sent into the world by the ambition of appearing in print, the apology has been, in order to deprecate the severity of criticism, that they were not intended for the public eye: and the authors of such books, after so candid a declaration, have generally thought themselves secure, without considering that the question would be put to them, "Why then do you publish?" On the present occasion, however, it will, it is hoped, be remembered that there is a species of writing, that has claimed, in all ages, the benefit of the apology, without being obliged to answer any further enquiries; and that is the epistolary style, which, if it be truly such, has a fair title to the exemption, as it cannot be supposed to have had the public in view, at the time of penning a letter to a particular friend. And yet such pieces have always been acceptable to the world, as men are best seen in those moments when they are least upon their guard.[16]

Baretti's defense for having "passed too frequently from my subject to myself" is based, as the author asserts, on the authority of Dr. Johnson:

In the descriptions that follow I hope it will appear that I have spared no pains to carry my reader in some measure along with me; to make him see what I saw, hear what I heard, feel what I felt, and even think and fancy whatever I thought and fancied myself. Should this method prove

---

[15] *A Tour to the East* (London, 1767), p. iv.

[16] *Letters Written from Leverpoole, Chester, Corke, the Lake of Killarney, Dublin, Tunbridge-Wells, and Bath* (London, 1769), pp. v–vi.

agreeable, and procure the honour of a favourable reception to my work, I shall owe it in a great part to my most revered friend Dr. Samuel Johnson, who suggested it to me, just as I was setting out on my first journey to Spain. It was he that exhorted me to write daily, and with all possible minuteness: it was he that pointed out the topics which would most interest and most delight in a future publication. To his injunctions I have kept as close as I was able, and my only fear upon this occasion, is, that some want of dexterity in the management of my narratives may justly have subjected me to the charge of egotism, as I am convinced that I have passed too frequently from my subject to myself, and made myself as much too often the hero of my own story. Yet this fear is not so predominant, as to exclude the hope that such an impropriety will be overlooked if I have but succeeded in the main point, and effectually assisted the imagination of my reader to form an idea tolerably just of Spain, by exhibiting as well the face of the country, as the manners of the inhabitants. This it will appear that I have laboured pretty hard to attain; and as this is the chief end of a traveller's narrative, the real critick will not be displeased that it has been principally pursued.[17]

In short, Derrick understood and Baretti learned from Johnson what generations of readers have demonstrated and some travelers have known—that, unless the narrative is animated by the experiences and personality of the traveler, the book will be dull reading and will not "effectually assist the imagination of . . . . [a] reader to form an idea tolerably just" of any foreign country.

In the preceding chapter it was observed how Smollett assumed the familiar manner in the *Travels;* when, however, he came to write *Humphry Clinker* with its fictitious travelers and hence could not appear in person, he identified himself in part with Matthew Bramble. The resemblances between Smollett of the *Travels* and Matthew Bramble of *Humphry Clinker* are numerous. Both characters are of the same age and suffer from much the same ill-health; both are skeptical regarding the efficacy of mineral waters and the pretentions of the medical profession; both are peculiarly sensitive in matters of personal hygiene; both have a hasty temper and a warm sense of personal loyalty. Yet all these correspondences do not imply that Smollett wrote his autobiography in his delineation of Matthew Bramble.[18] Further, though Smol-

[17] *Journey from London to Genoa*, pp. v–vii. (All italics in original.)

[18] Anderson, *Life of Smollett*, p. 133; Smeaton, *Tobias Smollett*, p. 96; Moore, *Life*, I, 140; Chambers, *Smollett*, p. 174; Saintsbury, *Humphry Clinker*, I, xi; Thomas

lett assigned to Bramble many of his own adventures and
many of his personal opinions, it does not follow that Smollett in similar situations responded as Bramble did or that in
his final tour of England and Scotland he underwent the
same ordeals. Bramble is rather an idealized portrait into
which went some of Smollett's traits, notably without the
Scottish inheritance, however, that was fundamental in
Smollett's character. The identity is, nevertheless, closest in
the Scottish episodes, and it was of these that Chambers was
thinking when he wrote:

> Smollett's last novel, published some years later—the *Expedition of
> Humphry Clinker*—was regarded by his relations as only a history, fic-
> titiously coloured, of his northern tour in search of health, and his resi-
> dence successively in Edinburgh and Glasgow. Looking back from his
> Tuscan retreat in 1770 to this last visit he was ever to pay to his native
> land, he—notwithstanding all present pains and troubles—seems to have
> revelled in the pleasing scenes of his early days which that visit had opened
> up to him, and in the recollection of the many kind and worthy people,
> old friends and others, whom it had enabled him to meet. He put himself
> in the foreground as the chief of the group of characters; he was Matthew
> Bramble of Brambleton Hall.[19]

Within the framework of the familiar letter Smollett inserted much material that normally went into a travel book.
He described Bristol, Bath, London, Harrogate, and other
localities visited on the tour and gave a long account of Scotland extending to nearly a sixth of the book. He expatiated
on contemporary English life and manners, including the
fashionable watering places, the sights of London, the levees
of courtiers, the intercourse of critic and author in the coffee-
houses, and all walks of life in Scotland from Caddy Fraser's
banquet to Douglas Hamilton's court in the Highlands. His
restless curiosity ranged over all sorts of subjects—Methodism,[20] the British Museum, public pleasure gardens, civil

---

Roscoe, *Miscellaneous Works of Tobias Smollett, with Memoir of the Author* (London, 1844), p. xxx; David Herbert, *The Works of Tobias Smollett, and a Life of the
Author* (Edinburgh, 1871), p. 40; and Scott, *Works*, III, 113. All the above accept
the identification except Saintsbury (*Humphry Clinker*, I, xi), who doubts it.

[19] Chambers, *Smollett*, p. 130.

[20] J. Albert Swallow, *Methodism in the Light of the English Literature of the Last
Century* ("Münchener Beiträge zur romanischen und englischen Philologie," No. 9
[Erlängen and Leipzig, 1895]), pp. 146–51.

justice, sea-bathing, architecture, painting, the adulteration of food,[21] the unsanitary conditions at Bath,[22] agriculture, commerce, Scottish scenery, and the manners of the Highlanders. The familiar vein in the travel letters of the age gave him license to include brief and, at times, generous allusions to contemporaries with perfect propriety and not, as Saintsbury has said, "with rather dubious taste."[23] To mention only a few, there are from England the Duke of Newcastle; William Taverner, the painter; Derrick, the author and master of ceremonies at Bath; and Charles Townshend, the Scottish chancellor of the exchequer whose repressive acts resulted in the American Revolution. In Scotland, Smollett celebrated Lord Elibank, wit and critic, who was friend and patron of many Scottish authors; Dr. Carlyle, then minister of the parish of Musselburgh; Dr. Moore, author of *Zeluco* and father of the lamented Sir John Moore; Dr. Gordon Smollett's old master in Glasgow; Commissary Smollett, a cousin; Mitchelson, a writer to the Signet, an office later held by Scott; Sir George Colquhoun[24] of Tilliquhoun, a lieutenant colonel in the Dutch service; and many others.[25] Most famous of all the portraits are those of Smollett himself in his prime as host to his hacks on a Sunday afternoon in Chelsea and of Quin in his declining days at Bath. Smollett knew Quin as early as 1739, when he began importuning

[21] Smollett's observations on the adulteration of food and drink were fortified if not prompted by several pamphlets that came to his attention as editor of the *Critical Review*. Among them are [James Manning], *Poison Detected: or, Frightful Truths* (London, 1757); Henry Jackson, *An Essay on Bread* (London, 1758); Emanuel Collins, *Lying Detected; or Some of the Most Frightful Untruths* (Bristol, 1758); Manning, *The Nature of Bread, Honestly and Dishonestly Made* (London, 1758); Peter Markham, *Syhoroc: or Considerations on the Ten Ingredients Used in the Adulteration of Bread-Flour and Bread* (London, 1758); *Critical Review*, IV (October, 1757), 296–98; V (January, 1758), 72–75; (May), 443–45, and *Universal Magazine*; XXI (December, 1757), 274–76. It was a rather interesting controversy, not without some humorous turns.

[22] Cf. Smollett, *An Essay on the External Use of Water*, ed. Claude E. Jones (Baltimore, 1935), *passim*.

[23] *Humphry Clinker*, I, viii.

[24] For the identification of the "Venerable Druid" (*Humphry Clinker*, II, 97–109), see Archibald R. Colquhoun, *Dan to Beersheba* (London, 1908), pp. 1–2.

[25] See Chambers, *Smollett*, pp. 126–72.

managers to accept *The Regicide*, and, although he resented
Quin's indifference, he admired his acting of Falstaff as he
disliked his interpretation of Brutus. Certainly Smollett
often met with Quin, and he was doubtless in Bath in 1766
when Quin died. In the resulting portrait Smollett not only
delineated Quin in his declining days as a voluptuary but he
also brought together many famous stories touching Quin's
life as an actor.[26]

For the abundant factual information included in *Humphry Clinker* Smollett resorted to the memory of his travels
and to an extensive acquaintance with books and men. As he
had done earlier in France and Italy, so when he traveled in
England and Scotland, he laid a solid foundation for his observations in standard books. In the course of his preparation of an account of Scotland for the *Present State of All
Nations*, he consulted the best books on Scottish travel and
checked and amplified what he read with firsthand observations. Quite naturally he availed himself of his knowledge of
England and Scotland when he carried the travelers in *Humphry Clinker* across the Tweed.

The excellence of *Humphry Clinker* lies, not in the descriptions which Smollett extracted from travel books or drew up
himself, but in the diversity in reactions of a group of travelers. One of the richest episodes in the novel concerns Bath,
long known to Smollett from frequent visits as well as from
his studies. His description of the resort, however, is not synthesized in the dry terms of a historian or geographer but is
dramatized in the lives of the imaginary travelers. Matthew
Bramble's violent reactions to the noises experienced while
settling in his first lodgings tell more of the clamor and confusion of Bath than all the parallel passages that Barbeau, the
historian of Bath, gathered from letters, diaries, and travelers' reports.[27] Tabitha Bramble's trials with her Laplander
cur Chowder,[28] Lydia's flutterings over the fashionable world,

[26] Some of the stories were to be found in *Quin's Jests or, the Facetious Man's
Pocket-Companion* (London, 1766).

[27] A. Barbeau, *Life & Letters at Bath in the Xviii*[th] *Century* (London and New
York, 1904), *passim*.

[28] An interesting parallel, or imitation, is to be found in Thicknesse's *New Prose
Bath Guide, for the Year 1778* (London, 1778), pp. 88–91.

and Win's encounters with the life belowstairs, each in complete accord with authentic records, dramatize in lively and concrete fashion conditions that were commonly experienced and frequently described. Similarly, isolated encounters become short commentaries on general conditions. This is mostly true in the parts of the book localized in Scotland, where Smollett presented Bramble's visits to friends, his meetings with strangers, and his tours as typical of Scottish life.

When Smollett set about developing the personalities of the travelers in *Humphry Clinker*, he turned for models to the fictitious travelers so tremendously popular with his contemporaries. In the pseudo travel letter the traveler was usually well educated but from a country whose simple manners were dissimilar and often superior to those prevailing in England or France, where he was traveling. Out of the contrasts which he observed between his own culture and that of England arose the material for the letters he supposedly wrote home to his family or friends. This device of describing England as seen through the eyes of a foreign visitor was in part suggested by Sorbière, Gemelli-Careri, Misson, Muralt, Baron de Pollnitz, Le Blanc, Voltaire, Baretti, and others, but more by the extraordinarily widespread interest in the visits of Laplanders, Indians,[29] South Sea Islanders, and the like brought to England by returning explorers and circumnavigators. In imitation of the actual foreign visitors, a widespread fashion for fictitious foreign visitors sprang up. Marana's tremendously popular *L'Espion du Grand Signeur* (1684–86), translated as *Letters Written by a Turkish Spy* and reprinted in twenty-six editions by 1770, and Montesquieu's *Lettres Persanes* (1721), widely read in Ozell's translation of 1730, stimulated if they did not originate the fashion.[30] Also in this group of pseudo travel letters of a foreign observer belong the English examples in Ward's *London Spy* (1698–1709), Brown's *Amusements Serious and*

[29] *Continuation*, V, 24–25.

[30] G. L. Van Roosbroeck, *Persian Letters before Montesquieu* (New York, 1932), *passim*; also Martha Pike Conant, *The Oriental Tale in England in the Eighteenth Century* (New York, 1908), pp. 106, 252, 262–63, and 285–86, for a discussion of Smollett.

Comical (1700), Hilliar's *Brief and Merry History* (1740), Lyttelton's superior *Letters from a Persian in England* (1735), Goldsmith's *Citizen of the World* (1762), and Shebbeare's *Letters on the English Nation by Batista Angeloni* (1756). The genre was still alive years later when, with *Humphry Clinker* in mind, Southey wrote his *Letters from England by Don Manuel Espriella* (1807).

Most eighteenth-century writers of fictitious letters, even if their attention was chiefly centered in travel material, endeavored in various ways to develop the national and individual peculiarities of their travelers and to increase the sense of authenticity by allusions to the personality of the recipients of the letters. Montesquieu introduced a slight story of Usbek's troubles with his wives, the unfaithfulness of his favorite Roxane, the death of her lover, and her suicide. Lyttelton has even less of a story in the love of Selim for Zelis. Goldsmith wisely did not multiply or expand Lien Chi's Chinese traits but instead introduced many Chinese short stories, allusions to Lien Chi's homesickness, and the love story of his son.

Smollett's travelers are not Scottish, whom the English disliked, or French, whom Smollett abominated, but Welsh, who were acceptable to the English and held in affectionate regard by the author. Although Wales was not so distant as Lapland or the Americas or Turkey or Persia or China, still in the mid-eighteenth century it was isolated and little explored, and the Welsh were almost as distinct from the English as were the Scots, French, Germans, or Italians. What Johnson thought of Scotland could be said also of Wales; a traveler "might there contemplate a system of life almost totally different from what we had been accustomed to see; and .... find simplicity and wildness, and all the circumstances of remote time or place, so near to our native great island."[31] By making his travelers Welsh, Smollett could thus contrast the "simplicity of manners in a remote part of the kingdom" with English life in London and the fashionable watering places.

[31] *Johnson's Journey to the Western Islands of Scotland and Boswell's Journal of a Tour to the Hebrides,* ed. R. W. Chapman (Oxford, 1924), p. 167.

Smollett added to the effectiveness of the pseudo travel letter by his use of a group of travelers all of whom report their experiences from different points of view. Matthew Bramble, M.P. from the borough of Dymkymraig, sees everything with the mature and slightly jaundiced eye of an elderly Welsh squire solicitous over his failing health; Jerry Melford is a young university graduate at home in the resorts of men; Jerry's sister, Lydia, watches the world of fashion; her aunt, Tabitha Bramble, is guided in all her observations by her pressing hunt for a husband; and Win Jenkins, the thoroughly provincial Welsh maid, describes English life from belowstairs. The original credit for Smollett's inclusion of more than one traveler goes to Anstey's popular *New Bath Guide* of 1766, a series of poetical epistles sent by the several members of an imaginary family to friends in the country, in which the several members narrate their experiences at Bath.[32] Once given the initial conception, Smollett's active and fertile mind developed the fictitious travel letter into a far more varied and extensive study of English and Scottish life. Matthew Bramble, to a greater degree than any of his party, injects his personality into almost every one of his observations, indulges in repeated personal allusions, and, as he is described by Jerry, Lydia, or Tabitha, so he in turn describes his family and retainers. Tabitha almost never pens a line without exposing another side of her greedy, restless, unhappy nature; and Win Jenkins injects one or another of her humors into everything she writes. The recipients of the letters, although their replies are not included in *Humphry Clinker* and only Miss Laetitia joins the party, are all more than names; Dr. Lewis, Sir Watkins Phillips, Mrs. Mary Jones, and Mrs. Gwyllim are as essential to the story as Humphry himself or Dutton or Lismahago. Out of the interplay of the several characters—Lydia's love for Wilson, Tabitha's pursuit of a husband, Matthew's concern for the

---

[32] The several parallels between the *New Bath Guide* and *Humphry Clinker* have been pointed out by Walter Maier (*Christopher Anstey und der "New Bath Guide"* [Heidelberg, 1914]) and Professor Knapp ("Study of the Final Period of Tobias Smollett," pp. 116-19). Many of the parallels are in subject matter and are to be expected when two men describe the same subject; others are more clearly borrowings, as the name "Tabitha Bramble" from Tabitha Runt.

fortunes of his friends, and Win Jenkins' vicissitudinous love for Humphry—grow the several plots logically evolved from the personal allusions of the familiar letter of travel. The travelers write to Welshmen, and they act and think as Welshmen. It is no exaggeration to say that the Welsh characteristics of Tabitha Bramble, Win Jenkins, and, in a lesser degree, Matthew Bramble and Humphry provide much of the savor of the book.

It is in the adroit handling of Lieutenant Obadiah Lismahago that Smollett most fully combined subjects peculiar to travel books and fictitious travelers. Like much that is excellent in Smollett, the character had its inception in personal experience, a short friendship with a Scottish professional soldier in the American service—Captain Robert Stobo. There is no way of knowing how much of his adventurous career Stobo unfolded to Smollett; it can only be assumed from Smollett's reference to the friendship that Stobo touched on most of the events in his life that have been recorded in historical documents and in the anonymous *Memoirs of Major Robert Stobo, of the Virginia Regiment* (London, 1800).[33] The source, the occasion, and the author of the *Memoirs* are not known. These deficiencies, coupled with the absurd style, do not predispose one to accept it as wholly reliable, and for this reason, except where noted, the ensuing sketch of the captain is taken from primary sources.[34]

Robert Stobo was born in Glasgow in 1727, the only son of William Stobo, an influential merchant and citizen, who at his death in 1740 left his son a comfortable estate. In the year of his father's death Robert enrolled in the university to study classics. He was not graduated but migrated to Virginia, where he prospered as a merchant, enjoying the favor

---

[33] Edited by N[eville] B. C[raig], with Introduction and Appendix (Pittsburgh, 1854). This is a reprint from a manuscript copy of the edition of 1800 in the British Museum (Introduction, p. xi).

[34] A search for primary sources has carried me far beyond the scope of this study. A full report of the findings will be found in the *Virginia Magazine of History and Biography*, XLIX (April, 1941), 141–51; *ibid.*, July, pp. 254–68. It has been necessary to reduce the extensive references to historical sources, which will be found in full in the article, and to give only the sources of quotations.

of another son of a Glasgow merchant family, Governor Dinwiddie.

In March, 1754, at the outbreak of the French and Indian War, Stobo enlisted in the Virginia militia, and, because of his enthusiasm and his friends rather than because of training or experience, he was commissioned a captain under Washington. The small army set out to seize Fort Duquesne but retired to Great Meadows in the face of a larger French and Indian force. Here on July 2 in a driving rain and behind embankments for which the *Memoirs* credits Stobo with the doubtful honor of acting as engineer, Washington and his men fought the Battle of Fort Necessity and were forced to capitulate. Captains Van Braam and Stobo were handed over to the French as hostages; but the terms of the capitulation were broken by both parties, and Captain Stobo became a prisoner of uncertain status in Fort Duquesne. Out of zeal for the English cause and a conviction of the perfidy of the French in violating the terms under which he was on parole, Stobo inspected the fort, noted the state of the defense, and reported his observations in letters of July 28 and 29, which he sent to Washington by two Indians whose confidence he had gained. Though he urged secrecy, the letters were circulated in Virginia until the French heard of them and thereupon refused to treat for an exchange of Stobo and Van Braam.

On September 20 the French set about transferring the two hostages to Quebec. According to the *Memoirs*, the journey was so protracted that Stobo had leisure to study the language and customs of the Indians, and in his friendly intercourse won for himself the "honor of the Mississaga Indian nation," the badge of which, in the form of a diadem, was tattooed with sharp fish-bones "on the foresides of both [his] thighs."[35] In the meantime his letter of July 28 was sent to England, brought back by General Braddock, and carried by him as he marched with his army on Fort Duquesne. On July 9, 1755, Braddock fell in a humiliating defeat, leaving

[35] *Memoirs*, p. 21.

behind Stobo's letter, which was found by the French in his baggage on the battlefield.

With this undeniable proof of Stobo's violation of his parole, the French confined the two hostages in prison and dispatched the letter to Paris for instructions as to what measures they should take. In the following year, 1756, the home government ordered that Stobo be tried as a spy and in justification of the action published a memorial which included Stobo's letter. The minutes of the trial have survived.[36] Captain Stobo conducted his defense ably and bravely, insisting that he was unacquainted with the code of warfare and ignorant of the duties of a hostage, that the French had violated the articles of the capitulation; further—and this was a point the court never refuted—that he confessed all his acts at Fort Duquesne to the commanding officers, Duquesne and de Vaudreuil, on the understanding that he would thereby be absolved of all guilt. He refused to take the oath of veracity and to identify the letter found in Braddock's baggage, whereupon the court called in a calligrapher who, examining a large number of manuscripts seized in Stobo's possession along with the letter in question, swore that all were in the same hand. The court accordingly ignored Stobo's defense, found him guilty of treason, and sentenced him to death.

Late in the autumn the warrant was sent to Paris for the king's signature. Before it could be returned in the spring, Stobo had made an unsuccessful effort to escape, and the English and French had patched up their differences, with the result that the death warrant was not signed and Stobo remained a prisoner. During his imprisonment, according to the *Memoirs*, Stobo fell in love with a "lady fair, of chaste renown, of manners sweet, and gentle soul," who addressed the Marquis de Vaudreuil as cousin. Who she was is not known; the *Memoirs* praises her for interceding for the Captain. The result was that the rigors of confinement were relaxed, and he was allowed to lodge on the ramparts. He took

[36] "Procès de Robert Stobo et de Jacob Wambram pour crime de haute trahison," *Rapport de l'archiviste de la province de Québec pour 1922–23* ([Quebec], 1923), pp. 299–347.

advantage of the privilege, however, to plot an escape with several other American prisoners in Quebec, and on May 1, 1759, with three men, along with the wife of one of them and her three children, he fled down the St. Lawrence River. It was a daring and eventful trip of twenty-seven days, during which they were shipwrecked, fired upon by armed French ships, and threatened with starvation; they set out in a canoe, captured a small boat, and later, after a skirmish, commandeered a large two-masted ship; they shot and scalped two Indians, seized a number of Frenchmen, and appropriated numerous supplies. Only after these and other daring exploits did they arrive safely in Louisburg.

Brigadier General Edward Whitmore, governor of Louisburg, was so impressed by Captain Stobo's knowledge and ability that he commanded a special boat to convey him back up the river to General Wolfe, who consulted him. Later Wolfe intrusted Stobo with leading the attack on Pointe-aux-Trembles. Three days before the landing at the Foulon and the battle on the Plains of Abraham, Wolfe sent Stobo with important dispatches to Major General Geoffrey Amherst, the commander-in-chief of the expedition against the French in America. On the way down the coast his boat was overtaken by a French privateer, and, in order to conceal his identity and to escape, Stobo threw his papers overboard and reached Boston empty-handed.

At the close of the campaign of 1759, during which he served as a volunteer under Amherst at Crown Point, Stobo returned to Virginia, where he learned that he was now a major and where he received a vote of thanks from the house of burgesses and a gift of a thousand pounds. On February 18, 1760, he embarked for England with letters of recommendation to those in power. Once again he fell into the hands of a French privateer and escaped with his life only by destroying his letters. He did, however, reach England and gain an audience with Pitt, upon whose recommendation he was commissioned on June 5, after his return to America, a captain in the Fifteenth Regiment of Foot, Amherst's own. As captain in the Fifteenth he was present at the surrender of Canada and was stationed in Quebec during the the winter of 1760–61. After seeing service in the West Indies under Major General Monckton, the Fifteenth returned to Canada late in 1763 and until early in July, 1768, occupied various posts. In June, 1767, Captain Stobo purchased a large parcel of land on Lake Champlain, the title of which was in dispute when the boundary between New York and Canada was negotiated in 1768.

The Captain did not settle in Canada but remained in active service. His regiment landed in England in July, 1768, and occupied various quarters in the southern and midland counties until the spring of 1771, when it marched into Yorkshire. Sometime before August 31, 1768, Stobo became acquainted with Smollett, who had lately moved from Bath to London. Under what circumstances the two came together is not known, but it is probable that these two Scots met in the London resort of the Scottish—the British Coffee-House. Smollett's generous words commending the Captain to David Hume are the finest estimate of Stobo's character that has come down from the pen of a contemporary:

> Perhaps I overrate my own consequence when I presume to recommend to your acquaintance and good offices, the bearer, Captain Robert Stobo; a man whose very extraordinary services and sufferings in America, have merited, and obtained the most ample and honourable testimonials, which he will gladly submit to your perusal. I can safely say from my own knowledge, that he is not less modest and sensible in the conversation and occurrences of civil life than enterprising and indefatigable in his military capacity. All these good qualities, united to an extensive knowledge of our American concerns, cannot fail to engage the friendship and regard of Mr. David Hume, from what quarter soever they may come recommended.[37]

In this letter Smollett does not intimate that he thought Stobo eccentric, conceited, vain, needy, or ambitious; rather he pays due tribute to the Captain's deeds and manners; also the tone of the letter suggests that Smollett enjoyed his company and the stories of his many extraordinary adventures. Hume replied in much the same vein from Ragley, September 21, 1768:

> I did not see your friend, Captain Stobo, till the day before I left Cirencester, and only for a little time; but he seemed to be a man of good

37 *Letters*, p. 103.

sense, and has surely had the most extraordinary adventures in the world. He has promised to call on me when he comes to London, and I shall always see him with pleasure.[38]

From the historical records Captain Stobo emerges with a somewhat neutral personality. There are only slight clues as to his appearance, habits, and opinions which Smollett knew full well and appropriated for the character of Lieutenant Obadiah Lismahago. On first appearance the Lieutenant is represented as riding into the inn court at Durham wearing "a coat, the cloth of which had once been scarlet, trimmed with Brandenburgs, now totally deprived of their metal, and he had holster-caps and housing of the same stuff and same antiquity."[39] In the closing scene when he approached the altar as a bridegroom, he wore a French coat of tarnished white cloth, faced with blue velvet and embroidered with silver, and a tie-periwig "in which he had made his first appearance as a lawyer, about thirty years ago." As gifts for the occasion, he presented to Matthew Bramble "a fine bear's skin, and a Spanish fowling piece," to Jerry "a case of pistols curiously mounted with silver," to Win Jenkins an "Indian purse, made of silk grass," and to his bride "a fur cloak of American sables."[40]

Could one have opened the trunks of Captain Stobo on his return from his American campaigns, much the same curious collection of clothes and spoils would doubtless have been found. Certainly when in 1757 the jailer made an inventory of his cell in Quebec, he found an array of personal belongings no less motley than those owned by the Lieutenant: trousers of close-cut white beaver, a mantle of beaver, fur-lined breeches, gloves of wolfskin, along with a suit of red satin lined with blue serge with alloy buttons, jackets of all colors, shirts of moire decorated with gold lace à la Bourgogne, scarlet trimmed with blue velour à la Reine and lined with white satin, a waistcoat of scarlet plush lined with fustian and with buttons of copper, a hat bordered with plumes, a diamond buckle for the neck, a garter of double ribbon of the

[38] Letters of David Hume, ed. Greig, II, 185–86.

[39] Humphry Clinker, II, 12. [40] Ibid., pp. 225–27.

color of rose, and a miscellaneous array of hose, shoes, gloves, toilet articles, pipes, and tobacco.[41] Allowing for the variety of colors and materials in the wardrobe of an eighteenth-century gentleman, one still has the impression that Captain Stobo had some original ideas regarding his apparel and that his wardrobe would have caught the attention of a bystander no less than the *opima spolia* of the Lieutenant.

Lismahago may have been indebted for his weather-beaten face and his meager, stooped figure to the Captain, who, after many a hard campaign on the American frontier, must have borne the marks of his service. His scalped pate, however, Lismahago did not owe to the Captain, for there is no record that he ever suffered at the hands of the Indians at Ticonderoga or elsewhere.[42] In fact, the remarkable feature of Smollett's characterization was his omission of all of Stobo's "very extraordinary services and sufferings in America" and his failure to take advantage of Stobo's "extensive knowledge of our American concerns"—all subjects of topical interest to Smollett's readers. What American experiences Smollett did attribute to Lismahago, he appears to have extracted partly from a "History of Canada," a serial that ran for over three years in the *British Magazine*,[43] and from the *Journal of a Voyage to North America* by Charlevoix as summarized in the *Modern Part of the Universal History* (Vol. XXXIX). Even though Captain Stobo may have learned

[41] [Pierre-Georges Roy], "L'Evasion de Stobo et de Van Braam de la prison de Québec en mai 1757," *Le Bulletin des recherches historiques*, XIV (May, June, 1908), 151–54.

[42] Captain Stobo was still in prison on July 7, 1758, when the battle at Ticonderoga was fought and apparently did not visit this territory until the autumn of 1759. Lismahago, on the other hand, fought at Ticonderoga, was left on the field and scalped by the Indians, but later revived and was cared for in a French hospital. What actually happened was this: the English furiously attacked the forts but were so fiercely repulsed that they withdrew in haste, leaving their dead and wounded on the field. On July 9 and 10 the French gathered up the wounded and treated them with care (*The Journal of Dr. Caleb Rea*, ed. F. M. Ray [Salem, 1881], pp. 31–32). Smollett is one of the few historians who declared that the French were assisted by the Indians (*Continuation*, II, 288–89); whereas the battle was exceptional in that no Indians participated (Joseph Tassé, "Un Point d'histoire," *Revue canadienne*, V [1868], 664–70). The defeat was much talked of in England, and Smollett was not dependent for his misinformation on Stobo. Stobo doubtless heard of the battle from Stevens, of Rogers' Rangers, who accompanied him in his escape from Quebec to Louisburg.

[43] Martz, *The Later Career of Tobias Smollett*, pp. 176–80.

First appearance of the gallant Lismahago

Rowlandson

an Indian language and studied the customs of several tribes, the information he passed on to Smollett was sadly confused. Lismahago dwelt among the Miami as a sachem of the Badger tribe, but "there is no known clan known as Badger among the Miami." Squinkinacoosta, the euphonious name of Lismahago's accomplished bride, if Algonquian (of which the Miami were a division), is "unintelligible as a genuine word."[44] Even Lismahago's resounding title, Occacanastaogarora, which Smollett thought signified "nimble as a weasel," is "pretty certainly not Algonquian," according to Dr. Michelson, but "is much more likely to be Iroquoian." Foster points out that, in his treatment of the American Indian, Smollett had in mind Shebbeare's portrayal of the Indians in his novel *Lydia* (1755); he calls attention to a number of parallels and suggests that "Lismahago's Indian name, Occacanastaogarora, is simply Cannassatego [the Indian in *Lydia*] made still more preposterous."[45] From whatever he learned of the American Indians, Smollett was obviously impressed not by their nobility but by their savagery. Of the progress of three Cherokee chiefs through all the sights of London, he had observed in the *Continuation:*

They saw all the improvements of arts and mechanics, the commerce, strength, and opulence of England, without discovering the least symptom of admiration, either in word, look or gesture. They seemed to be in a state of brutal insensibility, which indeed seems to be the character of the North American tribes in general, notwithstanding all the encomiums which some writers have lavished on the natural good sense and sagacity of that people.[46]

From this unfavorable opinion Smollett did not depart in *Humphry Clinker*.[47]

[44] For information on the accuracy of Smollett's Indian names I am indebted to Professor R. B. Dickson, who sent me to Dr. Truman Michelson of the Bureau of American Ethnology, Washington. The comments here quoted were communicated by Dr. Michelson in a private letter of February 4, 1933.

[45] "Smollett's Pamphleteering Foe Shebbeare," *Publications of the Modern Language Association*, LVII, 1076.

[46] *Continuation*, V, 25.

[47] Cf. Smollett's account of the death of a friend in the *British Magazine*, I (January, 1760), 19–20; *Critical Review*, VIII (October, 1759), 310–13; and *Continuation*, III, 192–96 [misp. 180]. In all three places Smollett repeats an anecdote of the brave death of Captain Ochterlony at the hands of the Indians at Point Levi, Canada.

Although Stobo's American adventures were such as might
be made good reading in a novel, Smollett was much more
interested in Stobo as a character. Fittingly, Smollett
changed the name "Stobo" to "Lismahago." The first is a
parish and village in the Lowlands from which presumably
the Captain's ancestors came. Twenty-five miles away in
southeast Scotland is Lesmahagow, also a parish and village.
Both parishes are on the road Lieutenant Lismahago must
have followed from Feltonbridge between Morpeth and Ber-
wick, in Northumbria, as he rode to his ancestral home in
Lanarkshire.[48] From either Stobo or Lesmahagow he naturally would have turned south to Dumfries, where he inquired
for his friends, and on to Carlisle without having to make a
circuit to Glasgow. Smollett's choice of a name for the Lieutenant was hardly fortuitous; the analogy would have been
quickly seen by all familiar with the geography of the Lowlands.

The similarities between the Captain and the Lieutenant
include also their families. It will be recalled that, upon his
revisit to the family seat, Lismahago discovers his nephew,
who has inherited the estate and is head of the family, engaged with his father-in-law in the spinning trade. Disgusted
with the mercenary spirit of his kinsman, he chastises the
nephew in wrath and departs to pass his declining days
among the Miami. Judging by the guild records of Glasgow,
Captain Stobo, also, appears to have had relations who became weavers and married weavers' daughters.[49]

Turning now from details of appearance, name, and experience to learning and character, one finds parallels increasing.
Lismahago "has had the benefit of a school education, seems
to have read a good number of books, his memory is tenacious, and he pretends to speak several different languages."[50] He seizes every opportunity to display his learning. For the origin of the nickname "Matt" he has an impos-
ing list of possible sources; elsewhere he quotes Latin, enters

[48] *Humphry Clinker*, II, 31, 38.
[49] *Burgesses and Guild Brethren of Glasgow 1573–1750*, pp. 415 and 471.
[50] *Humphry Clinker*, II, 15–16.

upon a learned discussion of the Scottish versus the English language, and concludes with some shrewd and entirely accurate observations on the problems involved in speaking a language that is not native. Before he has gone far on the road with his companions, he covers up a retreat from a losing argument by conceding that he has been bred to the law.

Captain Stobo possessed similar accomplishments. After a term or two of university study, which may have included law, Captain Stobo continued his reading and study even in prison. When he escaped from close confinement in Quebec in May, 1757, he left in his cell a collection of some twenty-five or thirty books, including Burnet's *History of the Reformation*, Josephus' *History of the Jews*, Marot's [*Œuvres?*], and Grécour[t's *Œuvres diverses?*], books on law, religion, travel, geography, military discipline, geometry, and, notably, grammars and dictionaries of French, Latin, and English.[51]

Lismahago's learning is associated by Smollett with the eccentricity of Don Quixote. He is by nature isolated in his thoughts, tenacious in his opinions, independent in spirit, and at variance with the world. Above all else, he is a Scot. In fact, he is the only fully developed Scot to be found in all the pages of Smollett; not even Roderick, Strap, or Micklewhimmen are such thoroughgoing studies in racial characteristics. Lismahago is not the Scot of law, medicine, the court, or the exchange; neither is he a raw clansman from the Highlands; he is the embodiment of the Scottish professional soldier, a figure familiar in the wars and armies on the Continent before the Union and after the Union in growing numbers among the ranks of the British army and navy.

Captain Stobo likewise was a Scot, a professional soldier, an individualist, and something of an enthusiast. By inheritance from his father he became a merchant, but, once given the opportunity to become a soldier, he showed that his natural inclination lay in that direction. Though commissioned a captain while still untrained and inexperienced, he had been scarcely six months in the army when he was able to appraise a military situation and plot a map that was accepted as au-

---

[51] [Roy], "L'Evasion de Stobo," *Bulletin des recherches historiques*, XIV, 152–54.

thoritative by Virginians, English, and French. His escape from prison in Quebec caused consternation among the French; Wolfe confidently relied upon his advice, and Amherst gladly made him a captain in his regiment. His rashness in intrusting his life to the fidelity of two Indians, only that he might aid in the capture of Fort Duquesne, his stubbornness and defiance during his trial for treason, his perseverance in his efforts to escape from prison—all sprang from a nature aggressively independent and a mind not always actuated by prudence and reason. In short, though Lieutenant Lismahago and Captain Stobo each expressed themselves in their own way, they were inherently alike in temperament.

Finally, both men in their maturity contemplated retiring to North America. Disgusted with the mercenary spirit of his Scottish nephew, Lismahago shook the dust of his country from his feet and set out for "North America, where he intended to pass the rest of his days among his old friends the Miamis, and amuse himself in finishing the education of the son he had by his beloved Squinkinacoosta."[52] Captain Stobo also must have talked to Smollett of his prospects in America. Mention has already been made of his large tract of land on Lake Champlain, which was in litigation while Stobo was in England. Also during 1768 and later he sought to establish his claim to nine thousand acres to which he was entitled as bounty for his services in the Virginia militia. Captain Stobo also had prospects, then, of a happy future among the Miami Indians in the Ohio Valley.

Thus it is apparent that, in utilizing Stobo as a source, Smollett ignored his adventurous career as a soldier but rather concentrated on his name, education, dress, habits, and temperament in the characterization of the Lieutenant. He subordinated the more commendable and attractive qualities of Stobo's nature—modesty, heroism, devotion to duty, and agreeable social graces—and, guided by a propensity for caricature, he accentuated the peculiar twists of his disposition. He transformed heroic perseverance into perverse captiousness; he distorted the honorable scars of hardship into

[52] *Humphry Clinker*, II, 118.

grotesqueness; he exaggerated the sense of isolation and disappointment into aloofness and pride. One trait he did retain—the Scottish fidelity to the Scottish motto, "Nemo me impune lacessit."

Smollett's artistic purpose in the characterization of Lismahago stands out in strong relief when his handling of Captain Stobo is compared with the treatment of the Captain by two later writers who also used him as a source for prose fiction. Captain Stobo's extraordinary American adventures, though largely ignored by Smollett, have more recently been fully retold by Sir Gilbert Parker in *Seats of the Mighty*, a best-selling novel of forty-five years ago. As early as 1873 Sir James MacPherson le Moine, the Canadian antiquarian, concluded a sketch of the Captain with the remark, "What a hero for a Canadian Novel!"[53] and it was at Le Moine's suggestion and with his assistance[54] that Sir Gilbert Parker wrote his novel, with Robert Stobo as a strong, brave, resourceful captain, later colonel, in the Virginia militia, hostage at Fort Duquesne and Quebec, a spy condemned to death, an intelligent aide of General Wolfe, and one of the leaders in the battle on the Plains of Abraham. Into the authentic background of historical events he wove an attractive love story of the Captain and the daughter of M. Antoine Juchereau Duchesnay, Signeur de Beauport. When Parker first published the novel serially in the *Atlantic Monthly*, he gave the characters their historical names, but later in the book he changed the names for no apparent reason, and "Robert Stobo" became "Robert Moray."[55]

It was not Stobo's adventures but his character as interpreted by Smollett that Sir Walter Scott seized upon when he created Captain Dugald Dalgetty, "Ritt-master Dugald Dalgetty of Drumthwacket," who occupied what critics and

[53] *Maple Leaves* (new [4th] ser., Quebec, 1873), pp. 55–63.

[54] *Maple Leaves* (6th ser.; Quebec, 1894), pp. 82–84 and 126–32; *ibid.* (7th ser. Quebec, 1906), pp. 370–87.

[55] *Atlantic Monthly*, LXXV (March, 1895), 289, to LXXVII (February, 1896), 198. Published as a complete novel, Toronto, 1896. See also Benjamin Matthias Nead, *Some Hidden Sources of Fiction* (Philadelphia, 1909), for a comparison of the *Memoirs* with *Seats of the Mighty*.

even the author felt was too large a portion of *A Legend of Montrose*. In this role he has been alternately called "one of Scott's bores" and "Scott's most humorous character."[56] Be that as it may, Captain Stobo, shorn by Scott of all his American adventures, becomes a soldier of fortune who serves at different periods under Gustav the Lion of the North and in the Dutch, Spanish, German, Cavalier, and Commonwealth armies. The adventures are of Scott's own making, but the character might almost have stepped out of *Humphry Clinker*. After acknowledging indebtedness to historical sources, Scott expressed his obligations to Smollett in these words: "In quoting these ancient authorities, I must not forget the more modern sketch of a Scottish soldier of the old fashion, by a master-hand, in the character of Lesmahagow, since the existence of that doughty Captain alone must deprive the present author of all claim to absolute originality."[57]

Sir Gilbert Parker welcomed Captain Stobo as a heroic adventurer; Scott through Smollett's eyes accepted him as a prototype of the Scottish professional soldier, but Smollett saw the adventurer and the professional soldier and more too—he perceived in Captain Stobo the potentialities of a humor character "with a method in his madness." Remembering that fools and eccentric veterans have generally been accorded the license to speak their minds without restraint on the most intimate and forbidden subjects and that they generally have won a hearing, Smollett created Lismahago as the great spokesman of a subject close to his heart and unavoidable in a tour through England and Scotland: a comparison of the English and the Scots. Elsewhere in *Humphry Clinker* the English and the Scots are generally kept separate and comparisons are only implied, but, once Lismahago comes on the scene, he renders an unrestrained verdict on all the delicate points at issue between the English and Scots that had been privately and publicly debated for generations.

[56] Andrew Lang, in the Introduction to his edition of *A Legend of Montrose* (London, 1893), pp. ix and xi–xii.

[57] *A Legend of Montrose*, p. xxvi.

For the material Smollett did not have to ransack books and periodicals. He needed only to recall his residence in London, his unhappy championship of Lord Bute, and his labors to present a fair survey of Scotland in the *Present State of All Nations*. What he did stand in need of was an original and engrossing traveler to vitalize the controversy, someone to animate all the points at issue between the two nations— preferment, language, poverty, oatmeal, learning, bravery, commerce, and the juries, the Union, the scurrilous libels of the English, and the freedom of the press.

In Lismahago, Smollett created a Scot who had lived long enough abroad to have become something of a foreign observer; though he was of Scottish origin, his long absence and his perversity prompted him to praise or condemn the Scots as often as he did the English. This eccentricity outweighed the bias of his nationality and placed the ultimate truth of his remarks on their inherent reasonableness. Smollett would not have been heeded even if he had been hardy enough to express his opinions on the contrasts between England and Scotland, while, on the other hand, Lismahago had the jester's license and was free to speak bluntly to both nations.

As a travel book, *Humphry Clinker* appeared most opportunely during the first great wave of travel through England, Scotland, and Wales; and Smollett's animated and original descriptions of the English and Scottish scene, the delight of later social historians, were welcomed by contemporaries as the staple ingredient of the book.[58] Of the half-dozen travelers mentioned in the first pages of *Humphry Clinker*, only Baretti, an Italian, and Derrick, an Irishman, made part of their tours in England. In the first half of the century there was little native travel in the British Isles, and, aside from numerous roadbooks, itineraries, and surveys, the number of travel books on England at all comparable in originality and imaginative qualities to the numerous books on foreign travel can be numbered on one hand. At the head

[58] See, e.g., the contemporary reviews in the *Critical Review*, XXXII (August, 1771), 81–88; *Gentleman's Magazine*, XLI (July, 1771), 317–21; *Town and Country Magazine*, III (June, 1771), 317–21; *London Chronicle*, XXIX (June 15–18, 1771), 580; and especially the *London Magazine*, XL (June, 1771), 317–19.

of the list is Martin Martin's unique and absorbing *Description of the Western Islands* (1703). In 1714–22 John Macky undertook to describe England and Scotland after the pattern of the Grand Tour in his *Journey through England, in Familiar Letters from a Gentleman Here, to His Friend Abroad* (2 vols.), and a third volume, on Scotland, appeared in 1723. Taking over Macky's plan and some of his material, Defoe, in 1724–27, from observations and books compiled his *Tour through the Whole Island of Great Britain*, long popular for its practical rather than literary qualities. Not until fifty years after Martin did another original and competent description of Scotland appear in Captain Edward Burt's *Letters from a Gentleman in the North of Scotland to His Friend in London* (1754), which in its day and down through the nineteenth century was deservedly popular.

Between 1760 and 1770, however, the tide of native travel began to swell. Thomas Gray visited the Lake Country and Scotland. In 1760 Richard Pococke crowned a career of adventurous foreign travel with a six months' tour of Scotland, and eight years later Arthur Young inaugurated his popular series of travel books with *A Six Weeks' Tour through the Southern Counties of England and Wales*, followed in 1770 by the four-volume *Six Weeks' Tour through the North of England*. In the same decade William Gilpin made the first of his "Observations . . . . relative chiefly to picturesque beauty," which he published some years later as *Observations on the River Wye and Several Parts of South Wales* (1782), the first of his popular series of five books on picturesque scenery. Finally, Thomas Pennant launched his career as a traveler with the first of his several excursions to Scotland, out of which grew his famous *Tour in Scotland* (1771).

In spite of the attention that had been given to Scotland as a result of the Union of 1720, the Rebellion of 1745, the unpopular Bute ministry, and the numerous books on Scotland, Johnson in 1773 apologized for his description of Aberdeen in these words: "To write of the cities of our own Island with the solemnity of geographical description, as if we had been cast upon a newly discovered coast, has the appearance of very frivolous ostentation; yet .... Scotland is little known to the greater part of those who may read these observations."[59] Smollett has Jerry Melford in *Humphry Clinker* make the same point with the remark, "What between want of curiosity and traditional sarcasms, the effect of ancient animosity, the people at the other end of the island know as little of Scotland as of Japan."[60] Walpole, whose reflections on Smollett and the Scots were warped by personal prejudice, comprehended at least part of Smollett's purpose when he described *Humphry Clinker* as "a party novel, written by the profligate hireling Smollett, to vindicate the Scots."[61] Smollett's "vindication" of Scotland was neither more nor less than a description of his country and a frank discussion, through Lismahago, of the traditional criticisms.

A disproportionate emphasis can be placed on Smollett's defense of Scotland. After all, the Scottish chapters take up much less than a third of the book, and, of this third, nearly a half is given over to Lismahago's animadversions. Readers less biased than Walpole remember the abundant descriptions of England and the entertaining humors of the travelers. Jerry Melford caught the pervading spirit of *Humphry Clinker* and of many a good travel book when he reflected at the end of their tour: "Without all doubt, the greatest advantage acquired in travelling and perusing mankind in the original, is that of dispelling those shameful clouds that darken the faculties of the mind, preventing it from judging with candour and precision."[62]

[59] *Johnson's Journey to the Western Islands*, p. 12.

[60] *Humphry Clinker*, II, 47; cf. also I, 85–86; II, 70–76. See also Henry Grey Graham, *The Social Life of Scotland in the Eighteenth Century* (London, 1899), I, 1–3, and Edward Burt, *Letters from a Gentleman in the North of Scotland to His Friend in London* (London, 1759), pp. 5–6.

[61] *Memoirs of the Reign of King George the Third* (London, 1894), IV, 218.

[62] *Humphry Clinker*, II, 206.

CHAPTER X

THE PROSE FICTION OF A TRAVELER

THE influence of travel on Smollett is discernible not only in a few characters, in separate chapters, and in the form of his novels, but also in his habitual methods of composition, for it was but natural that travel should have had a general as well as a specific influence. Smollett's imitators and critics all concur in recognizing his use of travel as a distinguishing characteristic.[1] His characters are usually strangers or travelers in novel surroundings. Roderick and Strap, Peregrine, Pallet, Fathom, Ratchcali, Sir Launcelot, and Matthew Bramble are all at one time or another traveling or adventuring abroad. With the exception of *Fathom*, the novels conclude with the return of the principal characters to their homes. In the last analysis Smollett imaginatively projected himself into many of the characters and scenes simply because he himself was an alien for most of his life and permanently retained the point of view of a traveler.

His social isolation as a Scot in London and the antagonism he experienced at the hands of the English left their mark on his novels. In the first place, most of his scenes have to do with public life—law courts, pleasure resorts, gambling halls, fashionable assemblies, theaters, coffee-houses, inns, taverns, and ships. Prisons in particular seem to have interested him, as they did many visitors to London, for he introduced a long prison scene into every one of his novels, the scene in *Fathom*

[1] Ernest W. Gray, "The Fielding-Smollett Tradition in the English Novel, 1750–1835" (unpublished dissertation, Harvard University, 1931).

148

Humphry Clinker in prison preaching to the Felons

being an almost purposeless digression.[2] No doubt Smollett's picaresque models had some influence on his choice of such scenes, but it is more probable that he turned to the picaresque writers because he felt akin to them in outlook.

In the second place, except for seamen, the majority of Smollett's English characters are brief sketches of one foible or another, each character bearing a name appropriate to his temper, habit, manner, appearance, occupation, or station in life. Only the Pickles and the Gauntlets approach anything like sustained portraits of Englishmen at home. Smollett, with less knowledge and sympathy than Fielding or Goldsmith, had an aversion to the typical English squire and in all the novels satirized him. Squire Bumper and Sir Timothy Thicket in *Roderick Random*, Sir Stentor Stile in *Fathom*, the drunken squire who modernized his ancestral portraits in *Peregrine Pickle*, Squire Sycamore of *Sir Launcelot Greaves*, and Squire Burdock of *Humphry Clinker*—all are portrayed with the same objective spirit of ridicule which Smollett displayed in his delineation of the French. Finally, Smollett carried his narrative through the English scenes and characterized his Englishmen with an air of detachment and a degree of objectivity which, though it cannot be described, may be perceived by comparing Smollett first with foreign visitors to England such as Muralt and Voltaire and then with native writers such as Addison, Fielding, and Johnson— a comparison that leaves little doubt that Smollett belongs with the foreign travelers.[3]

The fact that Smollett may never, consciously or unconsciously, have forgotten his Scottish origins and that he never completely and consistently identified himself with English life or lost his sense of isolation and detachment only enhances in one respect the value of his observations; for

[2] *Roderick Random*, III, 129–65; *Peregrine Pickle*, IV, 132–60; *Fathom*, II, 1–21; *Sir Launcelot Greaves*, pp. 218–38; and *Humphry Clinker*, I, 190–200.

[3] For many similar characterizations of the English by strangers see Edward Smith, *Foreign Visitors in England, and What They Have Thought of Us* (London, 1889), chaps. viii and ix: "Our National Character." Though Smith, being on the defensive, emphasizes only what is flattering, it is clear that Smollett was not alone in his strictures.

it means that Smollett wrote, as it were, from the vantage point of two cultures. John Shebbeare, introducing his fictitious Italian traveler Batista Angeloni, reviews the advantages of a detached point of view as they were appreciated by Smollett's contemporaries in these words:

> Like children, the natives are blind to the faults, and magnifiers of the virtues, which are inherent in their mother country; the sanguin mind exalting every virtue, conceives his nation the supreme of all, and invincible; the timid, uniting fear with love, is aghast at every apprehension of an attack from abroad, and trembles for his country; each of these from their native constitutions, where passions are strongly united with reason, are equally biassed to different and fallacious opinions, no true observation is to be expected from these men; and yet such form the generality of all nations. Thus then, a true state of any kindgom is not to be expected from the natives, either in its domestic police [policy], or foreign influence; for the same reason that the English are prohibited from seeing their national customs in a true light, strangers are equally prevented by prepossession in their own favour; besides this, they seldom tarry long enough in any country, to wear off the prevalency of first impressions, to be intimately acquainted with a people's manners, accustomed to their habits, and uninfluenced from particular prejudices.
>
> If ever they remain in any kingdom sufficiently to effectuate all this, they bid fairest to discover the real situation of it, to weigh its policy and religion with that of others, and draw the least partial conclusions.
>
> To know one country well, it is necessary to have long resided in some other; the medium which forms itself in the mind of man habituated to reflexion, cannot settle into the center of things, without being weaned from old customs by the habit of new; the loss on one side, and gain on the other, bring the ballance as near as possible to an equipoise.[4]

As a Scot on an English man-of-war, Smollett was inhibited from identifying himself with the seamen and from accepting the naval environment as normal or familiar. What to his companions were everyday occurrences he found strange, and he did not serve long enough to become in spirit and manners a sailor. As a result, he remained detached and observed far more than the men did who were habituated to the life. In a sense Crampley, Rattlin, Trunnion, Hatchway, and Crowe are not a seaman's but a landsman's conception of sailors.

Travel in all the ways in which it touched his work bred in Smollett a habit of mind that expressed itself in a surprising-

---

[4] *Letters on the English Nation* (London, 1756), pp. liv–lv.

ly large number of allusions drawn from travel books. He began with only a few in *Roderick Random:* banyan days and Indian sects, Moors of Barbary, the Cham of Tartary, Greenland, Greeks of the Morea, clime of Arabia Felix, and the orangutan. *Peregrine Pickle* adds to the number the "war whoop uttered by the Indians in North America," the river Dender, Negroes in Guinea who eat cats and dogs, Tavernier's account of Frenchmen on the Persian stage, methods of poisoning in India, the Gulf of Florida, and, best of all, the authority cited to substantiate the statement that Pipes drew sparks from the head of the poor Winchester gardener: "And let not the incredulous reader pretend to doubt the truth of this phenomenon, until he shall have first perused the ingenious Peter Kolben's *Natural History of the Cape of Good Hope,*[5] where the inhabitants commonly use to strike fire with the shin-bones of lions, which have been killed in that part of Africa."[6] Incidentally, Kolben's book is the source of Smollett's numerous references elsewhere to Negroes in Africa, in particular, to the Hottentots.[7] *Fathom,* the third novel, also contains allusions to the Hottentots as well as to Malaccans, Greenlanders, Algerians, Brahmans, Turks, and Spahis. The *Travels* is replete with allusions to Lapland, Guinea, South Africa, America, Turkey, Palestine, Georgia, Mingrelia, Egypt, and the "civilized inhabitants of Kamschatka," a range directly attributable to the knowledge Smollett gained in compiling the *Compendium* and reviewing many travel books. *Sir Launcelot Greaves* shows only a slight falling-off in comparisons with foreign lands, but in *Humphry Clinker* Smollett returns to his travel references with a new vigor.

Wherever such allusions are found, both in the novels and in the *Travels,* they demonstrate Smollett's abiding interest in comparative manners. Yet what is true of the literary allusions is even more true of his personal observations; wherever

---

[5] Translated by C. Medley (London, 1731), II, 95.

[6] *Peregrine Pickle,* I, 113.

[7] On Hottentots see also *Travels,* pp. 36, 57, 255, and 297; *Sir Launcelot Greaves,* p. 217; and *Humphry Clinker,* I, 21; II, 59.

he went, whatever he saw, and, at last, in whatever he wrote, Smollett was absorbed in comparing the national cultures of the French, Italians, Dutch, Scots, Irish, and English and in contrasting the lives of sailors and landsmen. From the time Roderick takes the highroad to London, through Smollett's *Travels*, until Matthew Bramble's return to Brambleton Hall, the subject is never dropped for long. Illustrations are too numerous to demand citation; one has only to glance through any of the novels or the *Travels* to appreciate how persistently this universal habit of other travelers has left its imprint on Smollett's prose fiction.

Lastly, there is a recognizable similarity between the style of travel books and that of Smollett. Defoe and Swift reflect the voyagers in their use of simple, almost colloquial vocabulary and a plain, direct narrative style, adorned or expanded by circumstantially detailed descriptions. Richardson, wishing to explore the motives of the human heart and to inculcate a moral at each new revelation, chose as his medium the dialogue or monologue for which he created a discursive, dialectical, colorless style. The style of Fielding, because it ranges from the mock epic to the colloquial, is not readily epitomized. It is the polished, balanced, detached, thoughtful style of an essayist—an elaborate style, rich in rhetoric. Smollett, on the other hand, evolved a style not for narration, analysis, or reflection but for description. With an abundance of material at his disposal, he was confronted with the task of selection and emphasis—a task in the solution of which he employed an idiomatic vocabulary without conceits or archaisms and a style marked by rapid transitions and objective clarity. This style was admirably adapted to conveying information of all kinds; when employed as a medium of narration, however, it focused attention on physical perceptions and shifted the emphasis in a story from the idea to the action. Much of Smollett's humor involves contrasts in manners and physical appearances, disparities of customs, incongruities between a traveler and his environment, and the activity of locomotion. In all such subjects the humor is more in the description of the physical associations than in the ideas or sentiments of the narrative. What applies distinctly to travel situations applies also to a considerable part of Smollett's other work. Again and again the appeal is addressed not to the intellect but directly to the senses and the emotions. It is undoubtedly this quality in Smollett's work that Thackeray had in mind when he said that Smollett "did not invent much . . . . but had the keenest perceptive faculty, and described what he saw with wonderful relish and delightful broad humor."

INDEX

Aberdeen, *Fasti Academiae*, ed. Peter John Anderson, 61 (n. 1)

Adam, Robert, architect, 75

Adams, Robert, 74

Addison, Joseph, 77, 87, 90, 97, 101, 107, 108, 117, 149

"Advice," the, 9

Akenside, Mark, portrayed in *Peregrine Pickle*, 42–49

Alemán, Mateo, *Guzmán de Alfarache*, xvii

Alexander the Great, legendary travels of, xiii–xiv

Allen, Robert J., *The Clubs of Augustan London*, 76 (n. 64)

Almeloveen, Theodore Jansson van, ed. Apicius, 45

Alvares de Cabral, Pedro, 82

Amherst, Geoffrey, Lord, 135

Anderson, Robert, *Life of Smollett*, xi, 40, 121 (n. 9), 125 (n. 18)

Annesley, James, 49–50

Anson, George, xx, 14, 15, 16 (n. 7), 74, 82

Anstey, Christopher, *New Bath Guide*, source for *Humphry Clinker*, 131

Antonini, Abbé, 97

Apicius, Marcus Gabius, *De opsoniis*, 44–48, 109

Appollonius of Rhodes, *Argonautica*, xv

Apuleius, Lucius, *Metamorphoses*, xvi, xix, 114

Armstrong, John, 74; *A Short Ramble*, 121 (n. 10)

Arnay, D', French antiquarian, 108

"Assistance," the, 9

Astley, Thomas, xx, 92

Atkins, John, 92

Atkinson, John, surgeon on the "Chichester," 4

Atlantic Monthly, 143 (n. 55)

Atterbury, Francis, 77

"Augusta," the, 18

Aulnoy, Marie-Catherine, Countess d', *Letters*, 106 (n. 21), 107

Babeau, A., *Les Voyageurs en France*, 111

Baldaeus, Philip, 82

Baltimore, Frederick Calvert, seventh Lord, *Tour to the East*, 122, 124

Barbeau, A., *Life & Letters at Bath*, 128

Barber, Francis, Johnson's servant, 68

Barbot, John, 92

Barclay, Patrick, *Universal Traveller*, 82, 83

Baretti, Joseph, 107, 129, 145; *A Journey from London to Genoa*, 55, 122, 123, 124–25

Battle of Dettingen, Smollett's references to, 37, 39

Battle of the Reviews, attack on *Critical Review*, 67

Beatson, Robert, *Naval and Military Memoirs*, 18 (n. 10), 19 (n. 13), 23 (n. 22)

Beaver, Alfred, *Memorials of Old Chelsea*, 77 (n. 66)

Bedford, John Russell, fourth Duke of, 74

Bélanger, Jean, "Note sur 'Roderick Random,' " 6 (n. 10)

Bennett, Arnold, *Journals*, 118

Bentley, Richard, 49

Berkeley, George, xx

Besant, Sir Walter, *London in the Eighteenth Century*, 76 (n. 60)

Bianchi, Giuseppe, 109, 111 (n. 33)

Binkley, Harold Cook, "Letter Writing in English Literature," 102 (n. 11)

Blainville, M. de, 97

Blair, Robert, 72

Bolingbroke, Henry St. John, first Viscount, 77

Bond, Richmond P., "Eighteenth Century Correspondence," 102 (n. 11)

Bosman, William, 92

Boswell, James, 75

Bovenschen, Albert, *Untersuchungen über Johann von Mandevile*, xiv (n. 3)

Bover, Captain John, naval career of, 28, 30–33, 34

Boyle, Charles, fourth Earl of Orrey, 49

"Boyne," the, 20 (n. 15)

Braam, Captain van, 133

Braddock, General Edward, 133, 134

Breton, Nicholas, 101

Breval, John Durant, 87